Living Today With Wisdom from Men of Old

LEARN HOW TO NAVIGATE LIFE WITH TIMELESS INSTRUCTION FROM MEN WHO HAVE BEEN THERE AND DONE IT!

Manny Donkor

First UK and World Paperback edition published by Manny Donkor

Copyright © 2024 by Manny Donkor.

First published 2024

The author's rights are fully asserted. The right of Manny Donkor to be identified as the author of this work has been asserted by him in accordance with the Copyright, Design and Patents Act 1988

All rights reserved. No part of this publication may be reproduced, distributed or transmitted in any form or by any means, including photocopying, recording, or other electronic or mechanical methods, without the prior written permission of the publisher, except in the case of brief quotations embodied in critical reviews and certain other noncommercial uses permitted by copyright law. For permission requests, write to the publisher, addressed "Attention: Permissions Coordinator," at the address below.

Manny Donkor 9, The Clay Farm Centre

Hobson Square, Trumpington

Cambridge CB2 9FN,

Cambridgeshire UK

www.ServingMyGeneration.com

mannydonkor@hotmail.com for general enquiries and book orders

Book Layout ©2017 BookDesignTemplates.com

The author's rights are fully asserted. The right of Manny Donkor to be identified as the author of this work has been asserted by him in accordance with the Copyright, Design and Patents Act 1988

Unless otherwise indicated, all scripture noted NIV is taken from the Holy Bible, New International Version 1987 by the Zondervan Corporation. Other scripture quotations are taken from the Holy Bible, New King James Version, 2001 Thomas Nelson Publishers.

Living Today with Wisdom from Men of old: Learn how to navigate life with timeless instruction from Men who have been there and done it! Manny Donkor.

ISBN 978-0-9569185-4-3

Contents

Chapter One Cloud of Witnesses 1
   Tim 1
   Sarah 3
   Jenny 5
   The Journey of Life 6
   Dynamics of Running a Race 13

Chapter Two: Gideon Mighty Hero 19
   The Meaning of Life 27
   Identity 28
   Philosophies, Institutions, and Systems 29
   Religion of Materialism 32
   In Summary 38

Chapter Three: Deborah When an Ordinary Woman Answers A Call 41
   Israel's Dark Period 43
   The Judge's Role 44

Chapter Four: Shiphrah and Puah Civil Disobedience 51

   The Dawn of a New Era 53

   Egyptian Infanticide 55

Chapter Five: Joseph Fulfilling Dreams with Integrity 63

Chapter Six: David The Shepherd-King 83

   Back-of-the-desert Experience 89

   Is There Not a Cause? 90

Chapter Seven: Nehemiah Owning a Cause 101

   The Wall of Righteousness 107

   The Wall of Justice 109

   The Wall of Identity 110

   The Task of Rebuilding 112

Chapter Eight: Esther You Were Born for Such a Time as This 121

Chapter Nine: Jabez Changing Destinies One Prayer at a Time 135

   Against the Odds 137

Chapter Ten: The Four Lepers Taking Risk Is Not Always About You 147

Chapter Eleven: The Hebrew Boys Stand Up for What You Believe 161
    The Spirit of Compromise 166

    The Golden Image 169

Chapter Twelve: Daniel Developing a Spirit of Excellence 175
    The Lion's Den 180

Chapter Thirteen: The Persistent Widow Persistence Pays 187

Chapter 14: Paul Discover Your Purpose 193
    Persecution without Measure 197

    My Damascus Moment 198

Chapter Fifteen: Equipped for Life 209

This book is dedicated to my mother, Joana Donkor, the woman who nurtured me into a man of purpose.

To my family and friends; thank you all for your amazing support and encouragement

To those who believe there is more to life than just merely existing; those who yearn to live a life of significance; this is for you!

Therefore, since we are surrounded by so great a cloud of witnesses, let us also lay aside every weight, and sin which clings so closely and let us run with endurance the race that is set before us, looking to Jesus, the founder and perfecter of our faith, who for the joy that was set before him endured the cross, despising the shame and is seated at the right hand of the throne of God.

– Hebrews 12 verses 1-2 (English Standard Version)

Chapter One
Cloud of Witnesses

Tim

Tim is a young twenty-six year old professional who, by modern standards, has a lot going on in his life. A rising star in a multi-million dollar company, he has the whole world at his feet. He is creative, energetic, and charming, always raising a few eyebrows among the ladies. He is the most eligible bachelor in town.

He delivers results when needed and has never failed to impress his company's top brass. Tim's meteoric rise to prominence is also receiving recognition in his community that helped shape his flair for success as more and more young men and women look to him for inspiration—a local role model and somewhat of a hero.

Tim represents many a young man's dream of living life to the fullest. But contrary to expectations both from the hierarchy of the company and the community, an internal battle rages inside of him—a battle to reconcile who he is and what he was created to be. This battle, on the surface, does not seem apparent as he churns out one success after the other when called upon. No one sees the turmoil inside.

When everyone has said, "Well done and congratulations" for another success, he will often go home, and alone in his closet, ask questions crying out from the depth of his soul—questions that make all of the success and accolades seem mundane and ordinary. He cries out, "Who am I? What am I here for?" Somewhere in the recesses of his soul, call it a deep, small voice or the real Tim, that keeps asking all of these questions that can only be answered by a deeper search for the true meaning of life.

Contrary to what people think or have come to expect, life as we know it is often not about churning out one success after the other; neither is it about the call we get into the CEO's office and the handshake we get when we receive a well-deserved raise.

Indeed, if life were seen only through the eyes of the pay raise or that big break we chase after, then Tim and many more like him would be the most fulfilled and satisfied people on Earth. It would be much easier for the world to have people who are satisfied with the level of life they live on a regular basis. This would make our planet a much safer and peaceful place to live. But this is not always the case.

Deep down, Tim struggles with what his life's purpose is. None of the achievements and accolades society showers on him provides the satisfaction he craves.

What would Paul the Apostle say to him about discovering one's true purpose? What would the man who had an identity change later on in his life say to Tim about how to discover and live a fulfilled life? Would he ever say something to him about the *Damascus moment* (a supernatural transformation) in a person's life and how to navigate through it in the context of living one's life purpose?

Sarah

What about Sarah? Who can quench the thirst in her life? As a teenager, she's learnt to get by through the hate she has developed for society; the very society which is supposed to nurture her into a confident well-rounded woman.

But before we quickly pass judgment on her, we ought to consider the circumstances responsible for nurturing her worldview— a worldview that is so common among many in an emerging generation. Sarah has never known the love and warmth of a family setting. She may have been given birth to by a mother and a father, but they have never been in her life. They are non-existent as far as she is concerned and perhaps rightly so.

Even though she is surrounded by friends who understand the value of family, she is convinced she was brought up not to have one. She does not have the security of knowing a family is there to support her as she goes through the various phases in life; that is, she does not have a father and mother who, within the secure family environment, can encourage her to dream about a better future, how to harness the potential she has, and assure her of unconditional love.

While the family unit typically serves as the place a young woman would be provided with cooked, healthy meals, hugs of comfort and encouragement, and affirmation from her parents, Sarah has never experienced that.

She does not know a parent's chastisement, especially from an authority figure assuring her and steering her into focus towards where she wants to go in life.

Instead, society has taught her a different set of values, while also shaping her worldview. She has learnt that her value and self-worth is perceived in terms of the pleasure she gives to people. To them, she is an object of gratification with no cause for dignity or self-worth. These are values reserved for the privileged few.

Society has taught her that she is the product of her upbringing and there is nothing that can be done about it. In its eyes, she will continue to feed off the system until she's served her time—and returns to her maker. As gruesome a picture as this may sound, there are a lot of people like Sarah in our world who yearn for dignity and decency in life.

Is there not a semblance of these fundamental human rights that one can live by? Certainly at some stage in life, you pause and ask some fundamental questions, especially when you see other people living a life that represents the norm. Surely, there is a standard of life; one far from the drudgery of the present circumstances which can be attained by every person—you do not need to be an archbishop of Canterbury or a sage to recognize this.

Yet, for all of this, there are those like Sarah who are constantly faced with these truths. How can they get out of this mess? How can they reclaim their human dignity and self-worth? I wonder what a biblical character like Jabez would say to Sarah.

Will Jabez's example of life provide her with the blueprint for her own rescue mission? There is one thing that is certain— an encounter with a strong, biblical character may well be what she needs to cause a drastic shift in her worldview.

Jenny

And there is Jenny, a young woman in her thirties whose dream has always been to hold a baby in her arms. She has always dreamt of becoming a mother. There is something about motherhood that seems to check all the boxes in her life. As a young child, she witnessed the joy of her mother as she nurtured, loved, and cared for her and her younger siblings. She became convinced as a result of what she had seen that her life's purpose and meaning could only be realised by becoming a mother and a parent.

Now this may seem a little awkward particularly in our post-modern, post-Christian, information age where women run boardrooms of multi-million dollar corporations rather than being domestic goddesses as society has tried to define them.

What a man can do, a woman can do better is the new slogan. And in case you are wondering, you are reminded that this is a post-Beijing era where the needs of a woman are of paramount importance. With all this said, all Jenny has ever wanted is to become a mother. This is not too much for an independent woman out there to ask, is it? She is an independent woman.

But this dream is fast disappearing before her as her biological clock ticks away. Instead of being so focused on her career that she has no time to dabble in matters of the heart, she has a healthy balance between career and her dream of becoming a mother.

Jenny has also been married for seven years to Joe who is as committed to her as she is to him. Because they are both committed to the same course, they have tried all the alternatives when it comes to having children, but they have proved elusive.

In fact, they are no strangers to the latest developments in the medical and scientific world where they have sought answers to the drought in their lives. And to make things worse, they are under increasing pressure from every side—family, friends, and even the unconcerned neighbours about what will happen next.

Out of their depths, I wonder what Hannah, the woman who went through barrenness, anxiety, and ridicule as recorded in Scripture would say to Jenny and Joe? Will they find comfort in her wisdom? Will Elizabeth's experience of finally giving birth to John the Baptist at an old age provide the hope they have lost in this ordeal?

The Journey of Life

Each of the people portrayed above are involved in what could be described as the race of life—a journey of long-term aspirations, but with short-term destinations.

While we may all not identify with the individuals described, as humans, we are all involved in a life journey. What we embark on can often be a corporate one where, with other people, we strive to achieve a common goal. Or as individuals, we often have dreams, visions, and aspirations we spend a large chunk of, if not our entire lives, aiming to achieve. Interestingly, those who do not fall into any of the categories mentioned often embark on a life journey of some sort, nonetheless.

Although someone's dream may not have been articulated, everyone embarks on a life journey by default. This is often the case where they see themselves mainly through the eyes of society. The prevalent mood, worldview, and societal attitudes are what they prescribe their life by. To prove this point further, let's illustrate a simple journey we all make every day.

When we run out of groceries at home, we restock the fridge and food storage, and this is often not by accident. It first begins with the realization there isn't enough food in the fridge or that the ingredients to prepare our favourite meal have run out. If we are frugal enough, we will draw up a list of items to be purchased and where we can get these items, especially when there are a lot of shops and supermarkets around, all vying for our hard-earned cash.

Now if you are a seasoned and prudent shopper, you will know which supermarket provides good, healthy foods at a bargain, and chances are that you are more likely to shop in that supermarket. Before you embark on the trip to the supermarket, you will have known where it is located and how you can get there. So when you hop into your car or take the public transport, you know exactly which route to take in order to arrive at the supermarket. If you take the bus, you would be influcnced by your destination so you would not board any other transport simply because it is the only one available.

Also, you would not board a bus that wasn't going to your destination. In the same way, even if Hurricane Ike is coming your way, you would not board the bus if it wasn't going to your destination. This is what happens in life.

When we want to go to the *supermarket of life*, we take the route that will eventually takes us to the premises. Those who board any bus that pulls up at the terminal without knowledge of its destination are likely to end up anywhere—in the desert where there is no life or among thorns or in enemy territory. And in such circumstances, the chances of surviving and going home in one piece are very unlikely, to say the least. This is why it is vitally important we have a definite destination for our journey.

Another way we can look at life is that it can be likened to a race—a race with a beginning and an end. Indeed, we often describe it as the *race of life*. And like a race on the track, we run with the sole aim of attaining a prize—to be crowned as the champion athlete. This is the goal of many athletes. Professional athletes run the hundred metres race with one goal in mind—to be crowned the fastest man on Earth and receive the money and prestige that comes with it.

Without a doubt, this is a goal worth pursuing. And in case you do not know, along with being crowned as the fastest man on Earth comes financial reward and the fame and publicity as added bonus. By now, you would realise that to achieve such an accolade is no easy feat, which is why athletes train hard for it. They often subject their bodies to rigorous exercises and a strict dietary regime. We have seen over the years the likes of Carl Lewis, Michael Johnson, Maureen Greene, Justin Gatlin, and Usain Bolt achieve this title. Many of them, though not in active sport, still enjoy the moments of fame and publicity for what they did in the past.

Similarly, life is a race which is run with much preparation and perseverance every day, month, and year of our lives. The fascinating thing about life as a race is it is not an exclusive preserve for the privileged few or muscular men.

It is something we all get to participate in, and it is the activity we will be pursuing until we have breathed our last breath. There is enough evidence scattered around which supports the concept of life as a race in which men partake. The most memorable and important piece of documentary evidence which proves this point is the Bible. Scattered in this book are references as far back to the pre-creation period where life was described as a race:

In the heavens God has pitched a tent for the sun. It is like a bridegroom coming out of his chamber, **like a champion rejoicing to run his course.**
Psalm 19:4-5 (emphasis added)

Do you not know that in a race all the runners run but only one gets the prize? Run in such a way as to get the prize. Everyone who competes in the games goes into strict training. They do it to get a crown that will not last but we do it to get a crown that will last forever.
Corinthians 9:24-25

I have fought the good fight, **I have finished the race,** *I have kept the faith.*
2 Timothy 4:7 (emphasis added)

Therefore since we are surrounded by such a great cloud of witnesses, let us throw off everything that hinders and the sins that so easily entangles and **let us run with perseverance the race marked out for us...**
Hebrews 12:1 (emphasis added)

So whichever way you look at life, one thing is clear—life is a race we run throughout our journey on Earth. You can run well and win the prize or you can run, but not so well, and end up losing out on the coveted prize. There are many men and women who have run the race of life before us. Some of them ran it well and won several prizes as a result.

These are the men and women we have grown to admire, some of whom we have never had the opportunity to meet as they embarked on their journey. I am quite sure that as you read this book, there are many people you may have come across either through learning about them in books and other media platforms as well as through word of mouth.

Dr. Martin Luther King Jr. is a great example of someone who ran his race and somehow won. He is the renowned American civil rights advocate who ran tirelessly in seeing that the American society accorded all of its citizens, regardless of their skin colour, the same rights and freedoms. In the first decade of the twenty-first century, we saw the fruits of his life's race when for the first time in its history, the people of the United States of America elected its first Black president in the person of Barack Obama. History was made on that fateful day when the poll was called in favour of the senator from Chicago. However, observers and students of history attribute this achievement to the tireless work of Dr. Martin Luther King Jr.

Another person we often admire is Nelson Mandela, the former president of South Africa, who worked hard to see the walls of racial segregation and apartheid gradually fall in that country. What was the price? It was twenty-seven years' incarceration. It was twenty-seven years of intimidation, all to force him to back down on his fight for the Black people of South Africa. And what was the fruit of his labour? He saw democracy firmly rooted in the country as he became the first Black president of post-apartheid, democratic South Africa.

Today, not only is South Africa a member of the free democratic world, but its advocate, Nelson Mandela, has come to symbolize the voice of freedom and reason. His exemplary life is an example many people admire and emulate. This is only because he chose to run his race well and attained the prize. Even though he is no longer with us, his legacy is still remembered the world over because he chose to run with perseverance the race marked out for him.

There are those on one hand who for one reason or the other did not run their race so well, and as a result, they missed out on the prize. Some of them paid a costly price for the way they lived their lives. I am quite sure you know a few people like this.

It is worth pondering on both types of runners and how they impacted their society. At this moment, I want you to close the book for a minute and ponder on those people you admire for the way they lived their lives and the impact they had on succeeding generations—the legacy they left in the minds and hearts of their communities. Do the same exercise for those who did not run their race so well—consider the pain and trail of devastation they left behind.

The men and women we've just talked about did not change their world or make a tremendous impact on society overnight. From what we have learnt, it is evident they planned, strategized, and took some actions that led to running a good race. Why would humanity be running the race of life towards a prize, yet some run well and attain it, while others fail to make it? Why would ten athletes, for instance, stand on the track; all with the same aim—to win the race and yet some run better and faster than others?

Like the ten athletes on the track, we all run with one thing in mind—to win the prize. Although the way we run may differ from one individual to another, what is it exactly that we are not doing enough of that is costing us the prize? And if that is the case, what could we do in order to attain it? How can we run the race of life and win? How can we make sure we do not repeat the same mistakes of those who ran before us?

Seated in the soul of every human is the desire for purpose and to work towards its achievement. Even those who do not recognize this often show signs of frustration and a lack of fulfilment—vital pointers to a life in desperate need of purpose. These signs often arise when we are not satisfied with the current state of life. However, it does not mean you are stupid or anything of that sort. What it simply means is that there is an inner struggle to reconcile who you are with what you were born to be. This is not always a nice place to be, but at the same time, it marks the beginning of a new life—a life full of meaning when explored further.

So how can we make sure we've got what it takes to run the race of life?

The secret lies in how well we plan and run our race or embark on our journey. Thus, to successfully run our race, we need to first acquaint ourselves with the processes, stresses, and pain of preparing, running, and winning.

Dynamics of Running a Race

We have all seen or heard men and women achieve great heights in any discipline whether in sports, academia, or politics just to mention a few. From Jesse Owens, Lionel Messi to Usain Bolt, Serena Williams, Naomi Osaka, and Nelson Mandela; we have grown to admire these exemplary people. Most often, what we do not recognize are the stresses and strains of preparing to win the race. For sports men and women, they often subject their bodies to sheer pressure in order to stay in shape for the race.

Behind the glitz and glamour, a lot of preparation by way of training and exercises goes into the making of a world record holder, not just in athletics, but also in other disciplines. The amount of exercise and training, both mental and physical, these sports men and women go through is one that many of us are not quite ready to undertake. And yet, these performers are very much aware that they need such a rigorous programme to be able to hit the mark.

In an interview at the National Stadium in Kingston, Jamaica, Glen Mills, the man responsible for the meteoric rise of the *bolt* attributed his protégé's success to what he describes as the three main ingredients—*passion, commitment, and dedication.*

Hang on a minute! You may wonder if you read that correctly—that with those three things, you can be on the way to becoming the next Usain Bolt? With those three ingredients, you can be well on the way to becoming a world record-breaking athlete at the highest level of performance?

This is easier said than done. And this is precisely true. Contrary to what Glenn Mills said, although that might encourage someone to jump into their jogging suit, it is not always as easy as you would believe. Behind each of those three words are actions, inactions, strategies, and the amount of hard work needed to achieve something in life, even when such goals are as lofty as becoming a world class athlete. There is no doubt there have been cases in which these people thought of giving up on the dream of winning the prize at some stage in their professional lives.

The sheer mental and physical torture they had to endure during the preparation stage is one they likely would have rather skipped if they had their way. But, they also recognize it is an important part in the journey to their future success, and because of this, they go through the pain. For them, the pain they experience often cannot be compared to the sheer joy and exhilaration that comes from achieving a goal—winning a race, setting a new world and personal best records, and the prestige it often brings.

This experience is often likened to the refining process that goes on to extract pure gold. The gold in its raw state undergoes intense heating usually twice the recommended temperature. This is done in order to remove the dross so that what comes out, is the real thing—gold in its purest form.

Similarly, when we, like athletes, go through the rugged terrains of training, we are able to recognize it is as an important part of the reshaping process all aimed at achieving our vision, a process we must go through in order to achieve our goal of finishing the race.

This includes, among other things, setting and meeting targets. Athletes commit themselves to a strict dietary programme aimed at ensuring they have the right nutritional balance. There is, however, one important thing they do which is vital, but often taken lightly.

This is not associated with the training and the other physical activities that come with aspiring to be a world champion. This aspect of the training has more to do with the athlete's mental build-up, where they acquaint themselves with the people of old who have achieved what they are aiming to do.

These people become their source of motivation even though some of them are no longer living. While some of the heroes may be in the same sporting discipline as they are, others are not. They are often people whose exemplary achievements provide the source of inspiration, confidence, and hope. But why would they read or watch the records of these people, some of whom they have never met?

King Solomon once commented that there was nothing new under the sun. In other words, everything we see today has already been. This is how he puts it:

What has been will be again. What has been done will be done again. There is nothing new under the sun. Is there anything else of which one can say Look! This is something new? It was here already, long ago; it was here before our time.
Ecclesiastes 1:9-10

Although the setting and context may have changed with the passage of time, the heart desires of man have not changed and neither has all the trouble associated with such achievements.

In the race of life, it is important to find courage and motivation from those who have gone ahead of us. In the book of Hebrews, the writer encourages us to run our race of life, looking up to those he describes as *a great cloud of witnesses*:

> *Therefore since we are surrounded by such a great cloud of witnesses, let us throw off everything that hinders and the sin that so easily entangles and let us run with perseverance the race marked out for us. Let us fix our eyes on Jesus, the author and perfecter of our faith...*
> Hebrews 12:1-2

We are encouraged to run the race marked out for us. What a statement! Each one of us has a race clearly marked out for us. It has your design specification on it—it was tailor-made for you and not for anybody else. It is sad to see many people live their entire lives without knowing exactly what they were born to do. As a result, many people die without ever discovering it.

For the living, it is often the case of living frustrated and unfulfilled lives. The passage encourages us that now, more than ever, we stand a better chance of living successful lives because we are surrounded by *so great a cloud of witnesses* whose life stories we learn important lessons from on how to do life—the wisdom we need to take those pivotal steps in life. And even for those who did not do well, we are provided a unique opportunity to leverage their mistakes to enhance the quality of our journey by skipping the potholes on the way to the destination.

We do not need to know them intimately in order to learn from them. They are all around us as the author of Hebrews assures us. If you want to be a successful business man or woman for example, chances are there are many people who have done things similar to what you are about to embark on and who can offer timeless principles, advice, and encouragement that will come in handy.

The book you are reading now is about some of these among the great cloud of witnesses. It is about these noteworthy ancient people who have gone before us. Their lives and interactions with the world and other human beings provide us with the blueprint for our journeys.

Consequently, in the next chapters, they will unveil some of the timeless wisdom and principles that allowed them to live their purpose or otherwise. But before we proceed further, you may wonder what is so special about these people—they are human beings just like you and me, aren't they? What is so special about what they have to offer us?

These are ordinary people who caught on to what they were created to do and who, as a result, were able to achieve extraordinary things during their time on Earth. They may not have been part of our post-modern, post-Christian, social media generation.

They may not have had the privilege to engage with the pressing issues of our time —issues such as global warming, terrorism, genetically modified food, and gender identity, among others. And yet, their experiences and life stories provide a road map for us. Their stories furnish us with the intelligence we need to live life to the fullest today.

Such is the potency of their life stories that it can hardly be ignored—you do so at your own peril. As human beings, we are often encouraged by the lives of those who have gone before us and the many battles they had to fight along the way.

So imagine for a couple of hours and under one roof, you are presented with the opportunity to hear first-hand accounts of the lives of these incredible men and women, many of whom we have heard, and in some cases, references have been made to their extraordinary life journeys.

This is not something someone is telling you. You are going to hear from the horse's own mouth; that is, we are giving them the voice to interact and speak to us almost as if they were with us today.

We have the rare opportunity to hear the likes of Joseph speak to us about destiny and from Gideon, the mighty hero! You should be excited about what you will hear. I am incredibly excited to hear all of these great men and women encourage us in our bid to live today with their incredible wisdom.

I can't wait as we unpack their extraordinary perspectives on life!

Worldviews will be shifted and realigned! Life will take on a different course after this encounter with these heroes of the faith! As trendsetters, there are vital life lessons about how to live today that they want you and me to know. Sit back and be encouraged!

Chapter Two:
Gideon
Mighty Hero

Our journey to live life using personal lessons from these heroes of the faith begins with a farmer. Imagine that you're in a room, with the stage all set. As he makes his way to encourage us, his demeanour becomes clear—he is a farmer with earth all over him. He also has a level of confidence about him as though he has something we will be interested in hearing.

The thought of a farmer bringing some much needed wisdom and encouragement seems intriguing enough as we begin to wonder who this man is; what can we expect from a farmer?

Is he in it to teach a thing or two about the latest advances in crop and animal husbandry? Or is he here to get more young people back to the soil? What can we possibly learn from a farmer about living life in a postmodern, post-Christian world? If anything at all, we are comfortable and safe in our digital, intelligent society! What more would we want from someone who is not from our world?

For what it's worth, we can't wait to hear him share his heart with us.

As we ponder on what we are about to hear, he comes towards us and begins to speak. He speaks with such authority as one who has seen and experienced a great deal; someone who has something special to share with us on how to live effective and productive lives.

For a moment, all the stereotypical thoughts we had about him gradually disappear. We become more excited to listen to what he has to say. And true to our expectation, he does not disappoint.

His first words unsettle us a bit—"*Mighty Heroes.*" *Heroes*? What has he seen in us that a wheat thresher should address us in such a patronising way? After all, we are still trying to find our feet in this challenging life journey, with some of us still struggling to find our bearing. We are in a constant battle to find that formula that will enable us to fulfil our purpose in life. He has no clue of the experiences and challenges we face on a daily basis. Thus, referring to us as *Mighty Heroes* makes us a little uncomfortable.

"You are all mighty heroes waiting to manifest," he repeats.

"Now, I know what you must be thinking while doing your lap on the field. I know you are perhaps wondering what must have prompted me to use those words. Or wondering why I would call you a mighty hero. Before I let you in on what I have to say, just accept what I have just called you because it is simply who you are!

"My name is Gideon, and I am here to share with you something important I learnt about myself many, many centuries ago. The revelation I got was that, deep inside me lies a hero simply waiting my recognition and manifestation.

"Yes, it is true, and I am a living proof of this!"

As he makes these comments, we cannot help but wonder what is to follow as we still grapple with the whole *Mighty Hero* issue; but at the same time, we are excited to hear what he has to say.

"I know you are still struggling with what I have just said, but don't worry because it will become clear to you very soon.

"You see, I have just said something which is mind boggling. This is exactly how I felt when I had the same thing said to me many centuries ago. I was, for all intense and purposes, a humble wheat thresher working in the field planting, nurturing, and harvesting what I knew and did my best ... except the period this happened in was a very difficult one in the history of my country—Israel.

"We had come under the brutal and oppressive dictatorship of Midian, a nation that had values and culture different from ours. Not that we had done them any wrong. Rather, our subsequent oppression and colonization was a direct consequence of our disobedience to God who was our protector and defender—He had been since the days of our forefathers.

"If you ever thought you were the only ones with questions about the sorry state of the world, think again! I had questions, too, way back then.

"Why would a God we've heard so much about, a God our forefathers spoke fondly of; why would such a merciful and loving God allow His people to go through so much oppression at the hands of a heathen nation like the Midianites? (Judges 6: 13)

"The answer is simple. As a people, we had broken the covenant God made with us through our forefathers in which He forbade us from fraternising with foreign gods. You see, our God is a deeply jealous God and wanted us all to Himself—such was the depth of His love for us. He was vehemently opposed to sharing us with other gods. He's still like that today!

"For our discipline, He gave us over to the Midianites. And such was the extent of our oppression by the Midianites. We became refugees in our own land, reduced to living in caves, mountain clefts, and such other places to keep as far away from our oppressors as possible. In fact, it is clearly documented in the Bible:

Again the Israelites did evil in the eyes of the Lord and for seven years he gave them into the hands of the Midianites. Because the power of Midian was so oppressive, the Israelites prepared shelters for themselves in mountain clefts, caves and strongholds. Whenever the Israelites planted their crops, the Midianites, Amalekites and other eastern peoples invaded the country. They camped on the land and ruined the crops all the way to Gaza and did not spare a living thing for Israel, neither sheep nor cattle nor donkey ... they invaded the land to ravage it. Midian so impoverished the Israelites that they cried to the Lord for help
Judges 6:1–6 (NIV)

"And this is where I came into the picture rather surprisingly. You see, when my people cried out to God for deliverance, He was not going to intervene personally as He had done previously. Prior to this period, we had enjoyed a period of peace and stability in our nation's history. We had forty years of peace from our enemies leading to a time of economic, socio-political development in our country.

"We were able to enjoy this season of peace and prosperity because we relied completely on God for sustenance. Prior to this period, He had commissioned a woman named Deborah from amongst us; a woman of great courage and virtue who led us into a great battle against our enemy, the Canaanites.

"So just as He had commissioned Deborah, He was going to use someone from amongst us to lead us into battle against our oppressors. What I did not know was that He had singled me out and actually prepared me for this very day and for this military campaign. But I had no idea. So far as I was concerned, I was anything but a warrior or a man with a military background.

"But God had something else in mind; something totally out of the box. As He's always done through the ages, He qualifies the unqualified!

"Looking at it today, it was almost as if I had a *real life* to live; a life quite different from that of a wheat thresher. This was why, like you, I had problems when I was addressed as a *Mighty Hero*. I was only a wheat thresher and not a man of warfare, leading me to believe that God, our protector and defender, had made a mistake in choosing me for what was obviously a massive military endeavour.

"I had no prior knowledge of modern warfare, let alone mapping strategies for dealing with such a fierce and brutal enemy as the Midianites. Besides, I thought of all the reasons why I was the wrong choice for this assignment, and they were all legitimate reasons.

"To begin with, I was the most insignificant person in my family. I had never done anything meaningful with my life up until now. On top of that, my family was the least popular among my tribe's people. There were no serious intellectuals or businesspeople or decorated sportsmen and women. There were definitely no decorated military veterans we could be proud of.

"In addition to this, my tribe's people were the least recognized in the entire nation of Israel. In fact, this was how I responded as is recorded in the Bible:

The Lord turned to him (Gideon) and said, "Go in the strength you have and save Israel out of Midian's hands. Am I not sending you?" "But Lord," I (Gideon) said, "How can I save Israel? My clan is the weakest in Manasseh and I am the least in my family."

Judges 6:14-15 (NIV)

"I barely knew how to use spears and swords; let alone using them in battle. There were a thousand and one reasons why I was the wrong choice for this assignment, and for once, I started to believe that God in his infinite wisdom did not know what He was doing—choosing the most unqualified person out of the whole nation of Israel. And so began my quest to talk myself and God out of the assignment by alluding to my lack of experience as well as my family background as indicated earlier.

"So when God said, '*Go in the strength you have and save Israel out of Midian's hands...*' (Judges 6:14), He was commissioning me to bring deliverance to the people.

"And I learnt a valuable lesson from that time on. When you are chosen and anointed by God to carry out a task, He equips you with the confidence, boldness, and the ability to accomplish it. This is mainly because you operate in God's strength rather than your own.

"After all, He knew a whole lot more about me than I did myself. In fact, He had already declared that:

Before I formed you in the womb, I knew you. Before you were born, I set you apart; I appointed you as a prophet (deliverer) to the nations.
Jeremiah 1:5

"In other words, unbeknown to me, He had intricately woven into my DNA, the skill of leadership with the capability of not only rallying people around for a common cause, but also the ability to put strategies in place to execute those causes.

"Now, although the primary aim of my commission was to rally the people in a united front against our oppressors, I soon realised the task ahead was much deeper and wider. At the heart of the commission were two main objectives:

"Firstly, I was to lead a nationwide purge of apostasy by pulling down and destroying all the altars erected in honour of the gods of the Amorites, one of our neighbouring nations. This was the wider task I had to deal with—reversing the apostate nature we had become associated with and then restoring the worship of the one and only true God—Yahweh (Judges 6:25-32).

"And then with that done, I was to spearhead a military campaign against our nemesis—the Midianites. This, as indicated earlier, involved rallying the people around so we could fight a good fight.

"The sheer magnitude of the task was such that I began to have serious insecurity and confidence issues. Therefore, I asked God for assurances that He had my back and that I was the right person for the job.

"Being patient and eager to commission me, God provided all the assurances I needed (Judges 6:17-22). It wasn't until I had received those assurances that I was able and confident enough to take on the challenge.

"In the same way, the culture you live in is in every way similar to what was happening back then. For some reason, you have all turned away from the virtues that have helped shaped your world. You have to take but a glance at the prevailing culture of the day to get a sense of the destruction, perversion, and cruelty being meted on a daily basis.

"And like me, you have intricately woven into your DNA, the grace and qualities by way of skills, talents, and abilities to 'go in the strength you have...' and rescue your families, communities, and your nation. The strength you have is very important to the rescue mission God is calling you to embark on. The strength He's given you will come in handy during those difficult and frustrating times when you feel like throwing in the towel; when you feel like *'this is just too much to carry, too much to bear.'*

"A look at your generation shows evidence which points to a broken generation—with all the freedoms and the pleasures, while at the same time, the gradual erosion of the tenets of what makes a healthy society are taking place.

"Just as it was in my time, there are many *altars of Baal* erected by your generation. These altars have been erected in recognition of the heathen gods of the world's system which often exalts itself far and above the God who created the heavens and the earth; the One who laid down the foundations on which our lives depend.

"And like me, He is calling you to the task of tearing down the elements of apostasy—altars your fathers built to the Baal of this world as well as pull to the ground the Asherah poles beside it.

"And in place of these, He asks you to erect a proper altar to the Lord, your protector and defender. Thus, your task is to pull down those strongholds over your generation and replace them with fundamental principles and foundations which have undergirded our lives for generations."

The Meaning of Life

"Since the beginning of creation, humanity has struggled to reconcile with its true purpose on Earth. Unfortunately, more than ever before, your generation struggles to come to terms with the issues surrounding the meaning and purpose of life. A closer look at your community or neighbourhood will reveal people running around, but with no specific destination.

"With all the technological advancement—inventions put in place to make lives much easier and better, many people are still at a loss as these safety nets have failed to fill the void. These advancements are not supposed to provide answers to the fundamental questions that remain core to our existence, but remain unanswered: *Who am I? What am I here for? What is my purpose?*

"Unfortunately, these questions have not been addressed sufficiently as more and more philosophies, systems, and ideologies emanating from human wisdom are thrown at humanity. You are the closest to the truth they will ever find.

"This is why like me, you are the most suitable candidate to bring the good news of the truth to your generation.

"You have been raised up to draw your generation back to the Architect of humanity. It is in humanity's return to God that true meaning and purpose emanate!

"This is what you have been called to do. Like me, you are the best suitable candidate for this task simply because right now, you are experiencing a radical change in the perception you have of yourself. You have the backing of heaven to accomplish this task."

Identity

"Back then, I struggled to come to terms with the fact that I had what it took to deliver an entire nation. This was because the nature of the crisis we faced required someone with authority; at least that is how I saw the situation. I did not know there was a hero in me awaiting my recognition and manifestation. This was because I had been conditioned to believe that my family and the tribe I came from were not good enough for the task set before me.

"Your generation, more than any other generation, grapples with the question of identity. The society rather than God places many limitations on people. The education system is often a culprit. Many lives have been grounded to a halt as a result of non-performance in achieving academic excellence. And while this is not bad in itself, these academic achievements do not encourage creativity where people can identify their inherent strengths, gifts, and talents.

"The system often says that one only has the chance to succeed if he conforms to standard procedures rather than by using creativity. Thus, for those who cannot follow procedures already laid out, they are deemed not to have what it takes to succeed. In other words, human criteria and limitations lower and often kill the potential of many men and women. This is why many people die, unable to express those hidden potentials. It nearly happened to me. I would have ended up dying as a wheat thresher, but God who knew me from my mother's womb spoke my potential over me. Just as He launched me, He has also endowed you with the strength to set your generation free from this crisis of identity; identity often carved along race or ethnicity, sexual orientation, and geographic, educational, religious, and social lines."

Philosophies, Institutions, and Systems

"There is no doubt that the establishment of institutions and a subsequent adoption of philosophies and ideologies over centuries have brought improvement to the lives of men and women around the world. However, this has not served humanity the way it was intended at creation. Rather than help answer many questions, it has created a genuine hunger at unprecedented levels; a hunger that has not been matched with credible answers.

"The adoption of a financial system which has greed as its premise is anything but fair and sustainable. Your generation has seen a great gulf between those who have enormous wealth and those who struggle to make ends meet. It is this disparity and greed you have been called to pull down and in its place erect a society based on equity and fairness in the distribution of wealth and resources.

"It is true that democracy has at its heart the inherent fundamental freedoms and liberties which rightly so, were given to mankind at creation. But what was meant to make life with God at its centre has been abandoned with a new emphasis on the individual as the core of its values. This has led to a battle about whether there is an absolute truth or not, or what has recently been described as the relativity of truth.

"This battle for the truth has fuelled a new generation of thinkers, ideologists who have sought to denigrate the truth about God's existence.

"Our forefathers had for a long period enjoyed absolute freedom and the liberties which came as a result of their covenant relationship with God. Under the covenant, He was their God—the absolute sovereign leader over their lives. Among other things, He would protect them against any aggression from both within and without. He was their provider; supplying them with everything they needed to make life comfortable. He even went as far as to provide food from nowhere as a way of demonstrating His love for His people.

"And to remove any traces of dictatorship or totalitarian tendencies, He gave them the power of choice—the ability of my people to do whatever they wanted to do as long as they were within His laws. And in return, they were to be to Him, a chosen people set aside purposely for His glory. They were to depend solely on Him for sustenance.

"This covenant brought harmony and absolute peace to the people of Israel. However, all of this was not enough for them as they strived to break away from the relative safety in a God who had assumed the role of ultimate defender of the people.

"They did this by rebelling against the freedom and liberties they had enjoyed. In a short period of time, they coveted the gods of the neighbouring countries they had struck alliance with, making them just like all the other nations. This is how the Bible documents one such event which occurred in Israel under the leadership of Samuel:

When Samuel grew old, he appointed his sons as judges for Israel. The name of the firstborn was Joel and the name of his second was Abijah and they served at Beersheba... so all the elders of Israel gathered together and came to Samuel at Ramah. They said to him: "You are old and your sons do not walk in your ways; now appoint a king to lead us such as all the nations have.
1 Samuel 8:1-5 (NIV)

"This proposal to be like all the other nations was not only a direct rejection of the authority of Samuel, who at the time was the direct representative and spokesman for God, it was also an outright rejection of God Himself.

"The result of the rejection was that everything went downhill immediately after that as they became prey to the neighbouring nations. Their source of strength and authority was lost, and they now operated in their own human strength and imagination—a dangerous thing to do.

"My ancestors continued to experience both economic and political turmoil right until the Messiah-King was sent to restore the peace we had enjoyed.

"Your generation bears semblance to the one I was part of in ancient times as you have broken ties with God. The brokenness and turmoil in your world today is largely due to your neglect and absolute denial of God's existence. You have been called to turn the hearts of your generation back to God."

Religion of Materialism

"Over the course of many centuries, your generation has erected another altar for itself—*the Altar of Materialism*. Your generation's obsession with material things is at a level never seen before in the history of humanity as we see men and women exert energy to acquire them.

"Sadly, we often pursue material things much to the detriment of our own sanity. Many centuries on, Jesus reminds us of the dangers of seeking and placing emphasis on material possessions when he said:

Watch out! Be on guard against all kinds of greed; a man's life does not consist in the abundance of his possession.
Luke 12:15 (NIV)

"This is the stronghold you have been called to pull down and in its place, build a new altar—the altar of generosity and contentment, among other things.

"These are the reasons why you exist, you *Mighty Hero!*—to bring the truth to your generation; to turn the hearts of people back to God and all that He represents.

"God in his infinite wisdom called forth my potential. The problem we were facing was the perfect opportunity I needed to exercise the authority through the gift and leadership qualities I had.

"God knows our strengths and weaknesses, abilities, gifts, and talents simply because He gave them to us in order to fulfil a definite assignment. We often do not use them because:

We do not recognize them.

"Every good and perfect gift comes from God. This is given to us when we are formed in our mother's womb. He has ordained us for a specific task, and in order to fulfil it, He puts within us gifts, talents, and abilities tailored for the assignment at hand. The only way to recognize this assignment and the resources He has provided for its completion is to ask him.

Remember, *"If any of you lacks wisdom he should ask God who gives freely and generously without finding faults..."*
James 1:5 (NIV)

These gifts and talents are for specific times and seasons.

"You also need to realize that these gifts and talents are for a specific time. Thus, you will recognize them when the time and season for its manifestation arise. I did not know I had these leadership qualities until this period of oppression. Looking at it now, I had been born for such a time as this. As Solomon later on points out:

There is a time for everything, a season for every activity under the heavens.
Ecclesiastes 3:1 (NIV)

"Just like it happened to me, when the time comes, you will rise to the occasion—it will be during this season that you will recognize you were born for a time such as this. So when you discover your gifts and talents, remember it is for a specific task and for a specific season. Do not be in a rush to exercise it straight away. Perhaps it is precisely the reason why I did not recognize my abilities until the appointed time.

We are often too busy with life to recognise the potential we have.

"Unfortunately, this is the human condition. Because we are so busy with the business of the world, we often do not recognize the potential we have, and then having recognised it, use our gifts to accomplish the task assigned to us.

"The result is many people live without a sense of purpose even though they may seem to achieve a lot by society's standards.

"When God calls you, He provides all the resources you need to accomplish the assignment He's given you. He also provides answers to all the questions and reservations you will have.

"Just as it was in my situation, He *clarifies all the doubts you might have regarding the assignment.*

"This is often in the form of assurances. He proves to us that it is all right to panic; it is all right to doubt in your ability to fulfil the task He assigns you. I had the same reservations (Judges 6:16). It only proves our human limitations, but also gives God the opportunity to show us what we do not know about ourselves, as He rightly pointed out to me:

> "*Go in the strength you have and save Israel out of Midian's hands. Am I not sending you?* "
> Judges 6:14 (NIV)

"He shows us He does not make mistakes in choosing us even though we may feel inadequate. In His own words, '*Am I not sending you?*' He is not sending anyone but you. The situation, difficulty, or crisis is one tailor-made for you and nobody else. You were born for such a time as this. You are the only one who has the solution to the problem. ARISE!

"He also shows us that we have the strength enough to accomplish the task He assigns to us. Even though we may feel inadequate, if we have strength as small as a mustard seed, we can still move those mountains. In other words, no strength—physical gifts, talents, and abilities are small or big enough not to be able to accomplish the task He has given us. Whatever the strength you have, it is enough to 'save Israel.' The strength you have is enough to accomplish what He has set out for you.

Having assured us, He provides the resources to accomplish the task.

"Because he formed us, endowing us with potentials, He is also aware of our shortcomings and weaknesses. So to ensure the assignment is accomplished, He brings people and circumstances our way to help us achieve it. One resource He provides is ourselves. He unearths the potential we have not yet uncovered. Right until now, I did not know I had leadership potential in me; I never thought that one day, I would summon an entire nation to fight a common enemy. But God knew before time that this would happen and that I would lead my country against our enemies.

"He will bring out your potential for the task ahead. You will then know the resources you have. He will also bring people your way. They are vision helpers. Because you cannot accomplish the task all by yourself in that you do not have all the expertise, He will bring men and women with the right abilities, skills, and attitudes to help you achieve the goal:

The Lord said to Gideon, "With the three hundred men that lapped, I will save you and give the Midianites into your hands."
Judges 7:7 (NIV)

"And in providing the resources, quality rather than quantity is important. Success often does not come from the quantity of the resources one has. The three hundred men I had for the assignment were strong and professional enough to bring victory to Israel. Besides, the whole campaign was orchestrated by God so that in the end, all the glory would go to Him rather than to men. God reduced the army from thirty-two thousand to three hundred men:

The Lord said to Gideon, "You have too many men for me to deliver Midian into their hands. In order that Israel may not boast against me that her own strength has saved her, announce now to the people anyone who trembles with fear may turn back and leave Mount Gilead ... three hundred men lapped with their hands to their mouth ... the Lord

said to Gideon, with the three hundred men that lapped, I will save you and give the Midianites into your hands."
Judges 7:2-7 (NIV)

"In the end, we defeated the Midianites without much effort mainly due to the fact that the strategy we devised worked perfectly well without us lifting a finger. My people were able to enjoy peace and prosperity; something they had not experienced for a long time simply because as a *Mighty Hero*, I was able to rise up to the task.

"In closing, I encourage you not to think of yourself as a nobody or a grasshopper. Remember, you are a *Mighty Hero* merely waiting for the season to be thrust onto the stage. If a wheat thresher is able to rise to his potential, doing exploits, then you can also fulfil your maximum potential.

"The world earnestly awaits the manifestation of your destiny! No eyes have seen; neither has any ear heard, what God is going to accomplish through you when you rise as a *Mighty Hero*.

"When you begin to walk in your maximum potential, the whole world will take notice of you. You will provide concrete solutions to the problems your generation faces.

"I release you to *RISE! MIGHTY HERO!*"

With these words, Gideon makes his way out of the tracks and out of sight. Faith and courage begin to well up inside us. As we reflect on what we've just heard, another "hero" approaches ...

In Summary

This is what Gideon wants you to know about living today from his life experience:

- We all are *Mighty Heroes* waiting for the opportune time to manifest our purpose (Judges 6:12).

- Your generation awaits your manifestation. You are what the world is waiting for, so arise and take your rightful place so your deeds may bring blessing and meaning to the world. (Judges 6:14)

- You are a person with a mission. Your mission is to pull down strongholds that exalt themselves above the principles and foundational wisdom on which our world has been built (Judges 6:25-32). Foundational strongholds such as secularism, relativity of the truth, and materialism should be pulled down.

- When God calls you with an assignment, He endows you with all the strength and resources you need. You have the ability required to accomplish the assignment. So *"go in this strength of yours"* (Judges 6:14).

- Remember, your assignment is for a specific time and season. Gideon did not know he had an assignment until his people cried out to God for deliverance. Remember, *there is a*

time and season for every purpose under the heavens (Ecclesiastes 3:1).
- Do not think of what you have to do. In most cases, God leads us towards what we need to do.
- He provides you with vision helpers who are loyal and dedicated to the task.
- Quality is often the key to the successful completion of the task, much more so than quantity. Gideon thought he was going to defeat the Midianites with thirty-two thousand men, but God had other ideas. He wanted three hundred men who would do the job better.
- Remember, the assignment is God's, and you are a channel for its fulfilment. He does this so that all the glory and fame will be His and His alone. It is not about you.

Chapter Three: Deborah
When an Ordinary Woman Answers A Call

Throughout human history, there have been a countless number of people who have risen to the challenges of the time. These heroes have dealt with those challenges by often harnessing their inner charisma in rallying people to accomplish the mission. However, rarely has the world seen a woman take the centre stage in leading the much needed change society so desperately requires, even if such change involves taking arms to fight a common enemy.

The next heroine of the faith to address us is one with unique insight into what it means to take the mantle of a leader and deliverer at the same time. Her story is unique when one considers the setting and demography of the period in question. Who would have thought that at a dark moment in a country's history, help would come from an unlikely source; a wife who is not your average woman.

The person in question is Deborah, the judge in Israel who played a pivotal role in redefining Israel's history, both spiritually and politically.

Deborah provides a picture of leadership that was not common in Israelite society at the time. In fact, very few women in scripture rose to positions of national leadership, thus breaking every glass ceiling at the time. Indeed, she stands out in scripture because of her role both as a spiritual and civil leader. She is the only female judge during a turbulent time in Israel's history.

She embodies what can happen when a vessel yields to the potter for the work that can only be accomplished by submitting. She is an example of what gets achieved when we heed to a call for a purpose higher and greater than we can possibly handle on our own. This is the woman of the faith about to speak into our lives.

What will she tell us about her time as the only female judge in Israel? What leadership nuggets will she hand to us? What will she tell us about how to live our lives today with wisdom?

As she makes her way down the tracks, we notice she is a woman of ordinary standing, yet a person who has witnessed and experienced much in her short life as a judge. There is an aura of authority surrounding her, making us eager to hear her wisdom on how to live today.

"I am an example of what an ordinary woman can achieve when she answers the call to rise and fulfill a mandate," she says. "Most times, it is when we heed the call that we come into our own, exhibiting gifts and abilities we never thought we had; or if we had them, they had been dormant up until now.

"As a judge," she continues, "I am privileged to have played my part in leading God's people into an area of peace and stability in the nation."

Israel's Dark Period

"The period during which I became a judge reflected a negative picture of my people drifting away from God spiritually and eventually experiencing God's judgment.

"After the death of my predecessor Ehud, Israel lapsed into apostasy (Judges 4:1). This was the pattern the Israelites found themselves in time after time which was in direct contravention of the theocratic arrangement between my God and my people. In it, the people of Israel were a special people to God while He assumed the role and responsibility of being their leader and defender, a role He jealously guarded. It is also worth noting that this arrangement was not a recent development. Rather, its existence goes way back to the time of the patriarch Abraham who walked blamelessly with God and who became the progenitor of Israel (Genesis 12:1-3; 15:1-26).

"This covenant has served as the basis for many a rescue mission for the people. Indeed, throughout the period of the judges, God continued to use the covenant to bring in men and women to lead his people in the right direction both morally and spiritually—that of undivided devotion to the one who had loved them with everlasting love.

"Another point in our history when he had come to our rescue was when we were subjected to oppression and servitude in Egypt. With the death of Joseph, there arose a Pharaoh who did not know Joseph and his exploits in Egypt. Thus, we were severely oppressed, so God sent a deliverer in the person of Moses to take us into a new period in our history where we would worship our deliverer and serve only Him. It was during this dark and turbulent chapter in our nation's history that God chose to use me to answer the cries of His people, who were my people, from the oppressive rule of Jabin, the king of Canaan. Jabin, together with his commander-in-chief Sisera, had inflicted much pain and hardship on my people.

"As a punishment for our apostasy, God would often *'sell'* us (Judges 4:2) into the hands of an outsider who would oppress us enough for us to cry out to Him in repentance. It is also worth pointing out that the scale of the slavery and oppression we were subjected to was such that there was no other way to get out of it than a heavenly intervention. The Canaanites had a strong professional army which had never been seen in the history of the known world. For instance, the Canaanite commander, Sisera, is reputed to have had nine hundred chariots fitted with modern weaponry for war. It couldn't have got any worse than that."

The Judge's Role

"As a judge, my role was three-fold:

Administration

Settlement of disputes

Providing military leadership

However, my role during this period in Israel's history evolved into one which involved spiritual awakening and leadership. Indeed, the title of judge in the Hebrew language indicated someone who would bring others into right relationship, thus pointing to a dimension of spiritual leadership.

As an Administrator

"As an administrator, my duties involved initiating and executing policies that would ensure Israel was heading in the right direction as enshrined in the covenant with God under a theocratic arrangement. I also helped settle disputes among the people to bring peace to the nation (Judges 4:5). As far as the people were concerned, there was an element of stability in Israel even though we were under an oppressive regime under Jabin and Sisera.

"It was, however, during this period of oppression which lasted twenty years that the people repented and cried out to God for deliverance. And the answer? Well, it was me!

"Stepping into the role unveiled a gift I had. I became an instrument in the hand of God to bring about the liberation we needed from our oppressor. The gift was prophecy, the divine ability to foretell what is to come in the future. I am described first as a prophetess, duly recognizing the gift I had been endowed with, as well as the wife of Lappidoth, my husband (Judges 4:4). Thus, the description was in a way, a recognition of who I was; a homemaker who also happened to be gifted with the ability to prophesy about future events. The presence of the natural (homemaking) and the supernatural (prophecy) became the instrument God used to redeem His people from their enemy. It was again symbolic of God's unconditional love for His people, so much that He was ready to use someone as ordinary as a wife, but with an incredible natural gift for His rescue mission. How loving can that be?

"So today, if you are wondering whether there is a purpose for your life, whether you have unique abilities and talents you can use for a greater cause, be reminded that there is a purpose for your life. You were created for a purpose. Contrary to popular opinion pervading in your culture, it is possible for an ordinary individual to rise to a greater cause. It is often in your rising up that untapped gifts and abilities become activated."

This exaltation is so much needed right now in our culture which only celebrates people for their "super human" qualities while denigrating the rest of society for not having such gifts and abilities. As a result, an emerging generation may struggle with issues of identity, confidence, and lack of self-worth among other things. If anything at all, Deborah speaks to the heart of many issues facing the emerging generation today.

Just as we chew over what she has said so far, she continues...

As a Leader

"As a leader, I came into my own when I received heavenly insight into how our liberation was going to come about. This led me into giving specific instructions to Barak, the commander of Israel at the time, about how to strategically position ourselves for victory. This is how it was recorded in scripture:

She sent for Barak, son of Abinoam from Kedesh in Naphthali and said to him, "The Lord, the God of Israel commands you: 'Go, take with you ten thousand men of Naphthali and Zebulun and lead them up to Mount Tabor. I will lead Sisera, the commander of Jabin's army with his chariots and his troops to the Kishon River and give them into your hands.'"
Judges 4:6-7 (NIV)

"At this stage, I was providing leadership for God's people by downloading heavenly military strategy for the assignment ahead. This was not me offering instructions based on human inventions and leadership philosophies. Rather, it was specific leadership instruction direct from heaven and quite specific, desperately needed for the hour.

"God, in His infinite wisdom, knew beforehand what would transpire, but was looking for an earthly vessel who would cooperate with Him to release His divine victory on the earth for His people. To further prove the divine nature of the instruction, I said, "The Lord, the God of Israel commands you ... (Judge 4:6b).

"Today, there is a 'the Lord, the God of Israel commands you' mandate on your life, and He is waiting on you to recognize this and to step out in faith. And it is when you heed the call that the provision you need will be made available. You don't have to be special. If a homemaker is able to rise to the challenge, then you can also do likewise.

"Even though Barak hesitated, the instruction which came forth proved so accurate that when it was obeyed to the letter, it brought about the annihilation of the Canaanites including Jabin and Sisera who had spearheaded the brutal oppression.

"In the end, because I yielded my life for God to use me, our land had peace for forty years; a long time in the life of a nation for the people to return to their God as He had planned from the beginning of time. During this period my people rededicated themselves to God as His people, pledging allegiance to live by His instructions."

We are encouraged by these words from a woman who was enabled to do extraordinary things when she heard the call to action in fulfilling a divine assignment. If there is one thing Deborah has taught us, it is that God is no respecter of persons, race, gender, and class. All He requires is a willing and yielding heart—that's all.

As we ponder over what we have just heard from a remarkable woman, she leaves us with these nuggets of wisdom to help us navigate life today:

There is a cause for which you are being prepared.

"One of the fundamental issues your culture faces is how to make the most of one's life, particularly when it comes to finding purpose. This is despite the fact that the culture has provided a lot of opportunities. Yet, many young people are unable to find out what their true life purpose is. I was a prophetess and a wife, but both roles became important when I yielded to the cause at hand—the liberation of God's people from brutal oppression. I did not pray about it; neither did I see a counselor to point it out to me. Similarly, a look around your neighbourhood, community, city, or nation will reveal a society falling apart from devising policies and programmes that are woefully solving the problems confronting society. And like me, there is a cry for judges who will yield their will to address the needs of society. Will you be the one who heeds the call?"

When we yield to a cause greater than us, it often unearths latent abilities and skills.

"You see, we have all been endowed with unique natural abilities and talents, some of which we are unaware. It is during times of national crisis that these gifts are brought to the surface in answer to the day's problems. This is what happened at this time in our nation's history. I was a prophetess. However, it was not until our crisis and God's intervention that this gift came alive. When I called for Barak and gave him the instructions, the specific nature of it suggested it was divinely-inspired rather than the product of man's effort. When you respond to the call of God about what is happening in your society, He gives you the strength and gifts to help you execute the assignment. In some cases, like mine, He activates latent abilities to help with the task at hand."

God uses ordinary people and things to accomplish extraordinary things.

"This is mainly so there will not be any human boasting; that all boasting points back to God. You see, if you consider all the men and women God has used to accomplish his divine purposes, you will notice that they are all people of humble backgrounds who are empowered by his Holy Spirit to achieve things only God-enabled, God-empowered life can do. Gideon, a farmer who struggled with confidence issues, was empowered to defeat a strong army in the Midianites. The four physically challenged men who will soon share their incredible story became the answer to severe drought and famine in which the people of Israel were reduced to a life of cannibalism. How did He do it? The footsteps of four crippled men! Never underestimate what God can do with an ordinary life that is completely surrendered to Him."

And with these encouraging words from such an inspiring woman, we continue with our race of life, brimming with confidence, that after such a time with a heroine of faith, we are ready to face the world head on.

Chapter Four: Shiphrah and Puah Civil Disobedience

Have you ever wondered what the repercussions would be if you went against the instructions given by your country's leaders? We are aware that obedience and respect for the laws of the land are our way of proving we are law-abiding citizens. But where do we draw the line when the laws we are required to obey conflict with our core beliefs and worldviews? Would we go as far as disobeying them knowing full well of the consequences of such defiance?

Two graceful women approach as we continue running our race of life. There is a great sense of defiance etched on their faces as though they have seen it all before; having gone against the current of popular opinion and escaping unscathed. It would be interesting to find out what their story is so we can also be inspired to take bold steps as we live productive lives in our modern culture. But before we encounter them, what do we know about them? For there is nothing of face value that gives us clues to their story, and yet, there is a sense they have had to dig deep to find courage, boldness, and tenacity to overcome incredible odds against them. This is what makes for a compelling reason to hear them out.

As we ponder on who they are, they approach us and begin to share their story of faith and confidence in their trust in God and how these elements were able to see them through a difficult phase of their lives which also mirrors the life of an entire nation at a pivotal time in its history. We can't wait to hear their story of sheer grit and determination.

As they begin to speak, we notice these women once worked as clinical people. They may well have been the first recorded account of nursing or midwives of some sort. But before we can clearly make them out, one of them begins to speak ...

"My name is Shiphrah, and we want to tell you that there comes a time in the life of every human being when they have to make difficult decisions; oftentimes conflicting ones as well as those that involve life and death. Whenever you are faced with such life-altering decisions, it always pays to make ones that do not conflict with your worldview and perspective. We are a good example of this."

This is such a life-changing experience we ought to pay attention. This is in view of the prevailing culture we live in where making compromises is the default position to take. It seems to be the most comfortable thing to do rather than one of defiance and swimming in the opposite direction. We are eager to learn more from these ancient women.

The Dawn of a New Era

The other woman continues. "We were midwives in ancient Egypt, who made the conscious choice to disobey the Pharaoh at the time and were vindicated by God. This decision was in reaction to the policy of the Egyptian king who wanted to get rid of the children of Israel through one form or the other.

"In going further, it is important for us to provide you with an insight into the prevailing conditions in Egypt at the time. We were part of a growing Hebrew population after we had been allowed to settle in the country through our ancestor Joseph. By divine promotion, he had risen from a Hebrew slave to becoming an important figure in Egyptian national life. He was made a powerful Egyptian Prime Minister when he drew up a plan to save the people from starvation.

"Unfortunately, upon Joseph's death and with him, that generation of great men and women who had a great impact on the country, there arose a new king who did not look with approval on the exploits of our ancestor (Exodus 1: 8). He hated the Hebrews and everything about us, the way we had settled into life in Egypt."

Signs of Prosperity and Success Among the Hebrews:

"Now, the historical account in the Bible (Exodus) painted a prosperous life for the Hebrews. Over time we grew wealthy in Egypt. This was not surprising considering the fact that what was unfolding in the nation was a direct result of God's promise to our forefathers—the patriarchs Abraham, Isaac, and Jacob. In fact, as far as I can remember from what my grandparents told us, God made a promise to our first ancestor that He would bless his posterity. This is how it was recorded in Scripture:

> "I will make you into a great nation and I will bless you. I will make your name great and you will be a blessing. I will bless those who bless you and whoever curses you I will curse and all people on earth will be blessed through you."
> Genesis 12:2-3 (NIV)

"God was, in effect, fulfilling His promise to His children and that's why we were wealthy.

"One area in which we were prosperous was procreation. We were fertile and productive in the number of children born into our community. In other words, we had many children, and this made us fruitful. As a result, we multiplied and became exceedingly numerous that the land of Egypt became filled with the Hebrew people. And this is what struck fear and panic among the indigenous people.

"They saw our multiplication as a threat to their sovereignty and national security. This would become apparent if there was an external invasion of Egypt by an aggressor. There was the genuine fear that we would join forces with the enemy to wipe out the entire Egyptian population (Exodus 1:8-10). Hence, the drawing up of policies of oppression and state-sponsored infanticide to curb what they considered to be the *Hebrew problem.*"

Egyptian Oppression and State-Sponsored Infanticide:

This is quite a dark chapter in the history of God's chosen people. Things couldn't get any worse than this as we chew over what has been said so far.

Puah continues...

"The Egyptians really oppressed us in the hope that we might lose hope of living and thus stop multiplying in number. They made life difficult, if not unbearable, for us. To dish out the most severe punishment on us, they appointed task masters who did not spare us at all. One of the results of this forced labour was the building of storage cities and granaries as well as depots for war provisions. *Pithom* and *Ramses* were two of such storage cities built during the period. However, they were not successful at killing our spirits in being fruitful and multiplying.

"Despite the severe hardship and brutal oppression, it did nothing to break our resolve as we defied the odds against us. Instead, the more they oppressed us, the more we multiplied and spread so much that they became afraid of us.

"I learnt an important life lesson from our situation: there seems to be an unwritten natural law that suggests that persecution serves to strengthen a people or a nation rather than break or destroy their resolve. Throughout human history, those afflicted or at the receiving end of brutal oppression tend to find ways and means of resistance until they become strong enough to fight back to regain their freedom. It is a known fact, as amply demonstrated by our situation, that persecution has caused a people or nation to grow and defy all the heavy yoke that had been put on their backs.

Egyptian Infanticide

"Seeing that they weren't making headway in their treatment of the Israelites, they decided to implement what could best be described as a deliberate state-sponsored infanticide; that is the killing of babies. This is where we came into the picture.

"We had been midwives leading our colleagues to offer much needed natal and post-natal care to Hebrew women. There was a total number of between five hundred to a thousand midwives looking after women and babies during and after childbirth at the time. This precious service became the latest tool for Pharaoh and his government to perpetuate their agenda of solving the Hebrew problem.

"We were summoned to the royal palace where we were given the order to kill baby boys of Hebrew women. This is how it is recorded in the Bible:

The King of Egypt said to the Hebrew midwives whose names were Shiphrah and Puah, "When you help the Hebrew women in childbirth and observe them on the delivery stool, if it is a boy, kill him; but if it is a girl, let her live."
Exodus 1:15-16

"This is where we faced the critical moment of making that life and death decision. We were aware of the instruction's source; we were even more aware of the consequences of not following through with the orders. We were also aware that what we did as midwives was part of a divine calling from God who was still our protector and deliverer. We had absolute reverence for the power and authority of God. Even though we knew what we were getting ourselves into, we were still able to go against the king's instructions.

"Simply put, 'we feared God and so did not do what the king of Egypt ordered us to do (Exodus 1:17), thus choosing to let the Hebrew babies, both male and females live.' And, as fate would have it, the nature of the birth by the Hebrew women was such that they needed minimal or in some cases no midwifery assistance to have their babies. The women would give birth before we arrived at the scene, so they did not need our help. As a result, we weren't able to intervene as much as we would have liked to. It appeared again that the plot to destroy God's people was successfully foiled."

This is an incredible story of sheer resolve and optimism in the face of accusation and painful death. However, in the mist of all this mounting pressure, they were still able to pluck up the courage to say no for a far greater cause.

How many of us in this generation will be prepared to go to great lengths to defy the ruler of one of the most powerful nations at the time? Or better still, how many will stick to their beliefs in the face of increasing pressure to compromise? Without a doubt, we owe a great debt of gratitude to these courageous women for standing up for what they believed in even if that means risking their very lives.

Shiphrah continues ...

"Suffice us to say at this point we were summoned to explain why the king's plan was not executed. This was our response:

"Hebrew women are not like Egyptian women. They are vigorous and give birth before the midwives arrive."
Exodus 1:19 (NIV)

"Thus, the oppression and hardships the Israelites were subjected to made them not only healthy and strong, but fertile which made giving birth easier, often with little or no help from a midwife. This chapter in Israel's history pointed to how involved God was in every detail of our lives. Although Pharaoh had plans to curb the Israelite population, we went on and the Israelites became numerous and also prosperous, defying all logic and human reasoning.

"Going against the king's instructions was anything but comfortable. We knew the enormous pressure, not to forget the grave consequences, which awaited us for taking such a stance. However, we were equally mindful of our heritage and considered what this would do to God's people. The consequence of defying Pharaoh's edict could not have compared to the surpassing danger of doing harm to God's chosen people. As a result, we were prepared to put our lives on the line by obeying our conscience and the reverent fear we had for God. We saw that as more important than any human threat."

These amazing women have, through their story, demonstrated how to stand up for our beliefs even if it means sacrificing our very lives on the altar of compromise and decorum. We need more of such people in our post-modern culture where the line between truth and falsehood is so blurred one can hardly notice the boundary. Perhaps, if there was ever a time we needed people to stand up for the truth of God's word in our culture, it is now!

We are so pumped up having heard such a remarkable story of resolve, determination, courage, and strength.

God Vindicates

With smiles on their faces, almost as if all the troubles they had gone through was worth everything, they continue with this incredible account of defiance in the face of hostility.

Shiphrah continues ...

"We did what we thought was the right thing to do, and this drew God's attention. God was pleased with us for not giving in on our beliefs that He rewarded us:

So God was so kind to the midwives and the people increased and became even more numerous. And because the midwives feared God, he gave them families of their own.
Exodus 1:20-21 (NIV)

"God blessed us by enabling us to have families of our own. This is what happens when we take a stand for Him. He never leaves us to fend for ourselves. This is what we want to leave with you. In your generation, God is looking for those who will stand up for Him in public; those who will recognise God as the ultimate saviour so as to put their lives on the line for Him. When you lay down your life for Him, you will gain it with so much more."

For one thing, Shiphrah and Puah have demonstrated that having a deep respect and reverence for God and His commandments rather than man's instructions does the following:

- It helps us to keep away from evil and not partake in sin (Proverbs 16:6; Galatians chapter verse 7).

- It prolongs life (Proverbs 10:27). Shiphrah and Puah, along with the Hebrew males, lived longer. Their fear of God kept them from the evils of contributing to the killing of innocent babies.
- It leads to riches, honour, life, and no lack (Proverbs 22:4; Psalm 34:9). This explains why God provided them with families of their own.
- It causes God to protect and deliver those who fear him (Psalm 34:17).
- It produces wisdom (Psalm 111:10). They managed to outwit Pharaoh without getting caught.

As they get ready to leave the race track, they offer us their final words of wisdom for the journey ahead.

"It is important to recognise that in our walk of faith as well as living purposeful lives in the world, you will be put in situations in which you have to make a choice about whom you will serve. This will affect everything else in your life. And it also influences how we live today. Would you obey and serve man thereby abandoning your fundamental worldview if your worldview aligns with God's will? In our quest to live purposeful lives, you must not abandon the beliefs you hold dear for popular opinions. Rather, you must be prepared to guard and defend these beliefs even if it means giving your life for it as we did.

"Usually, on the other side of the pressure, the near-death experience is a crown God lays out for those who have endured to the end. Our crown was having families of our own, but much more than that, there is a crown, an imperishable one, waiting for us in heaven.

"We see in the stands other heroes of the faith who have also endured right to the end and have received their crowns. We see Joseph, Daniel, and the other Hebrew boys who did exploits in Babylon. We have no doubt you are going to hear great life stories of how they overcame the odds which were against them. Learn from them!

"Lastly, the actions or inactions you take are part of a bigger divine purpose; something more far reaching than you ever thought. We simply made the decision and took action to go against Pharaoh in killing all male babies born to Hebrew women; not only was it against God's commandments, but we also saw it as a cruel act.

"However, our decision had far-reaching consequences. By not carrying out the king's plans, one of the many male babies saved later turned out to be the deliverer of the Israelites from Egyptian oppression and bondage. Even though we did not carry out his plan, Pharaoh was able to incite his people to carry out the killing of the Hebrew baby boys in the hope of achieving his goal, which was to solve the Hebrew problem. That is why a Hebrew couple who had a son hid him for three months because they knew he had a great destiny on his life (Exodus 2:1-10). Their son eventually became the one who delivered Israel from Egyptian oppression. Of course, we are referring to Moses.

"So when you make the decision to stand up for what you believe in, just remember that such a stance is part of a much greater cause to only be revealed later on in life. What may not be apparent to you is that a whole remnant of people are being liberated to walk in their divine assignment simply because of the decision you take to defend your beliefs and worldview. You should never forget that."

These are such encouraging and inspiring words we have heard from these amazing women about having the courage to stand up for what we believe even when fully aware of the consequences. We know this is what we need for the long journey ahead as we strive to live meaningful lives in today's culture. We will no doubt remember these resounding words for a long time to come.

With these words, Shiphrah and Puah give us a tap on the shoulder as they make their way into the cheering crowd to be followed by the next hero of the faith.

Chapter Five: Joseph Fulfilling Dreams with Integrity

After Shiphrah and Puah's inspiring message of encouragement, another hero of the faith steps out and approaches to speak to us. There is excitement in the air, especially after such an encouraging sword from the homemaker and prophetess.

We are God's answer to our society's call for reconciliation to Him. We are the answer to our generation, Deborah says. Shiphrah and Puah remind us to stand up for what we believe in especially when it clashes against the prevailing culture of the time. This is great stuff! We can't wait to hear what the next hero of faith will bring to us; timeless wisdom on how to live today.

The person approaching wears a white robe and what appears to be an Egyptian head dress. The name that immediately comes to mind is Pharaoh, the Egyptian king who oppressed the Israelites and opposed Moses prior to the exodus of God's people from the shackles of slavery. However, we know he would not be here to encourage us as he would have nothing to offer us; not a word of wisdom for our life journey, considering his track record and what he did to God's people.

Then it hits us!

This must be Joseph— the *love child* of Jacob and Rachel who went from a privileged son to the pits of slavery to the palaces of Egypt. As he draws closer, we notice he is the one who devised the ever-normal granary as a method of food preservation at a time of extreme famine and hunger across the known world at the time.

As he draws nearer to address us, we cannot help but wonder what he would say to us. Is he going to talk to us about the coat of many colours his father made for him, the coat that generated so much envy and hatred in his brothers? Or perhaps, he is going to let us in on his encounters with Potiphar's wife and how he was able to resist such an attractive woman.

As we keep guessing what he will want us to know about how to live our lives in our post-modern world, he begins to speak ...

"Your rise to greatness begins with a dream. It is the dream that will sustain you during the difficult periods in your life. But it is *integrity* that will take you closer to its achievement. So do not give up on your dream and definitely do not compromise on integrity, for pursuing your dreams with integrity is what God desires.

"Dreams are conceived long before they are achieved, and they are achieved by living a life of moral uprightness," he says.

"The period of time between the birth of a dream and its achievement is always a process. The process is often filled with naivety, doubts, adversity, challenges, changes, and surprises. During this period, you will experience good days and bad days. You will also be faced with a dilemma: whether or not the dream is worth the effort without compromises. Do I give up or carry on?

"Without hesitation, I can confidently tell you that when you come to this road, the simple answer is: don't give up and certainly don't give in on your dreams. They are the fuel that will keep the path to fulfilment burning. Many men and women have long departed the earth or lost hope simply because somewhere along the line, they compromised and subsequently, gave up on their dream. They easily gave up on the hope of one day seeing it come true.

Like the prophets of old, Habakkuk once said:

"Write down the vision (dream) and make it plain on tablets. That he may run who reads it. For the vision (dream) is yet for an appointed time;
But in the end, it will speak and it will not lie.
Though it tarries, wait for it;
Because it will surely come, it will not tarry."
Habakkuk 2:2-3 (emphasis added) (NKJV)

As we settle down to take in what he has said, Joseph wastes no time in imparting the wisdom he has learnt from a life of adversity, but also victory and fulfilments.

He continues:

Don't abandon your dream even if you didn't start off well.

"I did not get off to a flying start with the dream, but it did prove to be a lifeline during the difficult early stages of my life. I was a teenager, seventeen years old when I had visions from God that one day, my brothers and even my parents would bow down to me.

"Now, back then, this was a scary moment for me and certainly for my family. It was a difficult moment for them, too, as they tried to come to terms with the implications of the dream.

"You see, the beginning of a dream often generates more enthusiasm and less wisdom. For some naivety on my part and perhaps with enthusiasm, I made the dream public to my family in the hope that they would give me the needed encouragement and support. We often say things we shouldn't say or at that stage when it is premature to disclose. This is precisely what I did. The reaction I got for the dream was anything but good. It was mixed negativity which came from two sources.

"To begin with, my brothers were anything but excited about the whole idea of the dream. This added to the fact that they did not like me for a start. They hated me for various reasons; the dream being the last straw.

"Earlier on, I brought a bad report about their behaviour to our father which they didn't like. Secondly, being my father's 'love child' born to his favourite wife, Rachel, in his old age (he was ninety years old when I was born) gave me the reputation of Daddy's favourite child. My father even made a beautiful coat of many colours as a sign of my status among my siblings; something my brothers did not like.

"And such was the hatred I attracted that *'they could not speak a kind word to me'* (Genesis 37:4b). Thus they hated me 'all the more' when I had the dream which suggested I would one day be a great person.

"And the result?

"They plotted to have me killed so that in their own words, *'Then we'll see what comes of his dreams'* (Genesis 37:20b). The rest of what happened is history, but suffice me to say at this point that even though they wanted to get rid of me, God, who gave me the dream, had other plans—albeit a better one. And judging from my presence among you, He had not given up on me.

"On the other hand, my father, though initially thinking like my brothers, was the only one who did not take any extreme action towards me. Perhaps, he saw something other members of my family did not see; for while my brothers were jealous of me and wanted to take my life, my father 'kept the matter in mind.' He was not in a hurry to jump to conclusions concerning what would become of me.

"Similarly, like me, we sometimes do not start off well when we have a God-given dream or aspiration. And because of this, we often give up on them in the early stages when they are most fragile. I am encouraging you to recapture the dream you have abandoned and once again, own it.

"The secret here is we all have been given a dream; a vision to pursue, and true meaning and purpose in life can only be reached by discovering and owning them right from conception to fulfilment. And just like me, God is not ready to give up on you yet. Also for a dream worth its sort, it is very important that we exercise discretion on who we share it with. Not all skin folk are kinfolk!"

Don't abandon your dream even if your family doesn't support you.

"Dreams are like seeds which are sown in the hearts of men. They, among other things, possess a man rather than man possessing it. It is the dream that sustains you when support is not coming from anywhere. But be assured, that although there may not be help in sight, the One who gave it to you will always make provision and resources abound to you.

"When I told my family about the dream, their response was anything but welcoming. This is what my father said:

"What is this dream you had? Will your mother and I and your brothers actually come and bow down to the ground before you?"
Genesis 37:10 (NIV)

"I did not get any favourable response from my brothers either. Clearly, I wasn't going to get any support from anyone in my family. Your dream can often make you the *last man standing*. It can be lonely and isolated to be a dreamer, especially when those you expect support from do not understand what you are pregnant with and, as a result, withdraw their support. Thus, it makes it difficult to retain your dream when those closest to you would rather have you release it from your mind.

"Compromise is the only option left!"

"But when your dream is divinely inspired, it sustains you when you feel inadequate. When the strength you have is gone as a result of the challenges you face, the best solution is to throw your hands in the air and settle into a life of mediocrity and be average.

"But that is when you need to persist; for challenges are indications you are about to birth forth your baby—the vision. So do not give up nor give in."

Ultimately, it is your dream that will guide you through the journey full of surprises.

"In pursuing your vision, things may not always go according to schedule. There may be many detours along the way which will cause you to doubt the long-term benefits of the journey and whether it is worth pursuing. In some cases, what you experience will not be according to the script.

"But just because things don't go according to plan doesn't mean you should give up on them. This is what separates the real visionaries from the *'others'* —those who are simply in it for the ride and often coil up very quickly into their shells when things do not go according to plan—and those who actually pursue and get things done.

"Now, looking back on my journey, there were a thousand and one reasons why I should have given up. These reasons were genuine and legitimate enough for one to end any worthwhile pursuit. Let's have a look at a few of them:

"*I was, first of all, misunderstood by my family.* That was enough reason to give up. They were the closest to me; they were my flesh and blood, and yet they did not understand the vision. This was circumstantial enough to merit my acquittal from the race of life.

"But I did not! Many of you will go through this experience as you run with the vision God has given you.

Just like me, you cannot give up because your generation is awaiting the fulfilment of your dream since their deliverance and well-being depends on its fulfilment. Therefore, if you give up, not only will you be abandoning your purpose, but more importantly, you will be destroying the destinies of other people with you. Your purpose is intrinsically linked to theirs.

"If the family rejection was not enough reason to quit, then being sold into slavery is without doubt a clear reason to back out of the race. Living in a foreign country was hard enough to take, but living as a slave proved to be the last straw.

"I was taken away from my country, my community, my family, my culture, any semblance of normal life, and most importantly, my faith. This was not an easy place to be in. Imagine for a moment how it felt to be uprooted from familiar surroundings to an alien culture and the shock of it all!

"Some of you may be in situations in which everything resembling human dignity is stripped away from you. You may be at a point in your life where you think that nothing will ever come of the little seed you are nursing.

"Perhaps, the power of choice which is an innate quality of life has been taken away from you. Do not despair and neither should you give up on your vision, for in due season, you will receive the promise if you hold on.

"Looking back on the journey, I can confidently say that I had my great-grandfather's genes which made it a lot easier to cope with the disappointments and difficulties I experienced on the journey.

"My great-grandfather Abraham provides us with a classic example of how not to give up on the promise. He went through a similar situation when God called him to start a new breed of what would ultimately become the peoples of the earth. It was difficult because like me, he had to leave his comfort zone.

"The Bible records this about him:

The Lord had said to Abram, "Leave your country, your people and your father's household and go to the land I will show you" ... so Abram left as the Lord had told him.
Genesis 12:1-4 (NIV)

"It was as a result of his obedience to the vision of God that we came into existence because, as part of God's bigger vision, 'all people on earth will be blessed through him.'

"Following in my great-grandfather's footsteps, I did not give up because I knew that at some point in my life, humanity's destiny would be fulfilled through me. You should also not give up even though you are very uncomfortable right at this moment because you are out of your comfort zone. I would also echo what the writer of Hebrews says:

So do not throw away your confidence, it will be richly rewarded. You need to persevere so that when you have done the will of God, you will receive what he has promised.
Hebrews 10:35-36 (NIV)

"Sexually tempted and wrongly accused, I could have been bitter about how unfair life had been to me. Instead, I chose to walk in integrity and not compromise on what I believe is moral and true.

At this moment, there are giggles as we ask ourselves these questions: *Did he really do it? Was it easy for him to say no to Potiphar's wife?*

With intuitive anticipation, Joseph prepares to give an answer after a long pause. "I know you are dying to find out whether or not I slept with Potiphar's wife. But herein lies the secret I want you to know.

"I was a very handsome guy at the time; something a lot of women would have found very difficult to resist. Besides, I was a slave serving in my master's house; away from my family and country. I was a foreigner. It would have been easy for me to get involved intimately with my master's wife since he concentrated all his energy and effort on the affairs of the Egyptian state.

"I had nothing to lose since by my estimation, the dream was anything but fulfilled.

"Furthermore, she was a very beautiful, attractive woman. As the wife of one of the most powerful men in Egypt, she was not deprived of the very best the richest and the most powerful country had to offer. Perfume, expensive clothing, and all of life's trappings were at her beck and call. She took good care of herself, thus making her difficult to resist.

"But here is the key—*Integrity and righteous living enabled me to not give in to the amorous advances of Potiphar's wife.*

"I was able to run away from her, leaving my cloak in her hand because I didn't want to sin against God and my master. Besides, I had a God-inspired dream, and giving in to her sexual desires would amount to a serious compromise. It would have meant selling my birthright for a bowl of lentil soup as my uncle Esau did previously.

"The easier thing to do at the time would have been to enjoy my moment of pleasure; I could have cared less of some dream about stars and the moon bowing down to me. If there was any shred of evidence as to whether it would come to pass, why would my own flesh and blood sell me into a distant land as a slave?

"But I did not give in to these legitimate questions. Though I did not quite understand what was happening to me, I was mindful of the dream which at this stage was like a seed planted in the soil of my mind, heart, and soul, waiting for the right time to spring forth. This is why I had to maintain my integrity. This is why when she asked me to *'come to bed with her,'* I comfortably declined adding that:

"... my master does not concern himself with anything in the house; everything he owns he has entrusted to my care.

No one is greater in this house than I am. My master has withheld nothing from me except you because you are his wife. How then could I do such a wicked thing and sin against God?"

Genesis 39:7-8 (NIV)

"I had a responsibility to my master and most importantly to the One who had infused me with his dream-seed. So contrary to what people believed, it was very easy for me to walk away from what was clearly a moment of pleasure. The consequences would have been too expensive to pay.

"Your generation seems to have lost its position and authority on Earth primarily because they have not learnt to walk away from the world's pleasures. Many have fallen prey to the *moment of instant pleasure and gratification* the world promises. But as they have later found out, the cost of such glory is very expensive—for some, it has caused both physical and spiritual death.

"Dreams and visions, many of which have been planted in our hearts by God have been missed. As a result, many have lost out on the enormous potential of seeing lives changed and destinies fulfilled all because they could not resist temptation and other such obstacles which prevented them from entering into their purpose.

"You have to nurture the dream in you and be prepared to maintain your integrity in your journey to its fulfilment. Your dream and integrity are the currencies you have to negotiate for a better future. Do not abandon them!

"In pursuing the dream God lays on your heart, you have to be prepared to resist the enemy of your soul, and when you do this, he will back away from you.

"When you decide to stand up for purity and integrity, you are most likely to come under intense persecution and pressure. When this happens, do not abandon your dream.

"I was thrown into jail because I would not give in to the amorous advances of my master's wife (Genesis 39:11-23). She wrongly accused me of trying to seduce her; even to the extent of trying to forcibly have sex with her when, in fact, it was the opposite. And even if I was angry and frustrated with the situation I was in, God used my time in prison to work on my character in preparation for the dream's fulfilment. In other words, I was still convinced the dream would come to pass, and it would take a life of integrity to rise to the top.

"The time in prison was a learning experience for me as God used it to prepare me for the season which was about to unfold. He was always there with me even when it didn't seem like it. The favour I had with the prison guards and the servant heart I developed in attending to Pharaoh's officials, the cupbearer and the baker, were ample evidence of his divine protection and preparation.

"Looking back on all the trials and difficulties I experienced, I can confidently say that it was the prospect of having the dream fulfilled that sustained me throughout the ordeal.

"Many of you may be in seasons where you think the challenges of life are too difficult to handle. Like me, it is not there to punish you; neither is it there to break you down. Rather, it is there to build you up for what lies ahead, which is something great. In these seasons, ask God to give you the strength to go through it (Jeremiah 33:3; James 1:5-8).

"In God's grand scheme of things, I was scheduled to go through this fireproof exercise all in preparation for what laid ahead—to save God's people.

"So whatever experiences you face at the moment, it is all in preparation for the glory about to be revealed in you and through you. But you will have to first go through life's refinery where your character is shaped before you are brought into your purpose. What you are experiencing now, like me, is all not in vain."

Joseph has so much to say to us and so little time to share. But as he wraps up, he offers us these words of encouragement:

God is always with you.

"It is especially important to remember that during the toughest times, when no one seem to care about what is going on in your life, that God is with you as He was with me and all the mighty men and women before me. When I was lying in the pit, I didn't give up hope because deep down, I knew God was watching over me. He did keep my brothers from killing me (Genesis 37:19-36). And when I was tempted by Potiphar's wife, I also knew God was with me, giving me the strength to say no to her.

"But far from that, He gave me the strength to overcome temptation. Remember my friends, that in trials and temptations, God is with you, too."

Develop yourself during the difficult times.

"When you suffer injustice and hard times, often complaining doesn't do you any good. When life's circumstances get you down, the best thing you can do is allow it to make you a better person.

"The king's officials I was with in prison forgot to mention my name to the king after I had received assurances from them that they were going to bring my case to Pharaoh's attention as one of the people to be granted a royal pardon. But I did not allow the situation to get me down. Each time I found myself in trouble, I tried to learn something new. You must try to do the same."

Realise that self-promotion can never replace divine promotion.

Each time I tried to promote myself, it worked against me. I thought I was going to count on the officials to clear my name, but it did not work out. Look at what happened when I told my brothers about the dreams—they hated me even more and tried to take my life.

"By the time I appeared before Pharaoh, I had finally learnt my lesson. I knew that my success came from God—and I gave Him the credit. The only advancement that mattered is the one God gave."

Trials and tribulations serve to bring the best out of us.

"As I discovered, we often do not realise the incredible potential in us. It is only when we commit ourselves to the fulfilment of God's purpose that we unearth these abilities He has given us.

"Prior to this period, I had dreams, but never had the ability to interpret them until Pharaoh had a series of dreams which could not be interpreted by any of the seasoned astrologers in Egypt. I discovered during this period that God in his infinite wisdom had given me this incredible gift of interpreting dreams. It was the gift that eventually brought me into my destiny.

"And the result?

"I went from being a Hebrew boy serving as a slave in my master's house to becoming the Prime Minister, effectively making me the second most powerful man in the land—only second to Pharaoh."

Dreams realised are sweeter than can be imagined.

"When what you have is God-breathed and God-given, its fulfilment is worth the wait. Do you know what it was like to finally reconcile with my family after many years? There were times I thought I would never see them again. As it turned out, the whole situation was divinely orchestrated ahead of time and for a greater purpose.

"God knew what lay ahead and destined me through the dream to prepare us for what was to come. He knew there was going to be famine in the world, and at some point, my people were going to die of starvation; so He destined before time that I would come to Egypt in a bid to preserve His people. I was to be the answer to the problem. This is why I finally plucked up the courage to tell my brothers:

"But as for you, you meant evil against me but God meant it for good in order to bring it about as it is this day, to save my people's lives."
Genesis 50:20 (NKJV)

"As a boy, I dreamt only of power for my own gain. But over the course of thirteen years, I came to realise that the dream had a far greater purpose than what I had thought it was for; it wasn't about my ego at all. By God's grace, I was able to save my family, live on prime land, and head the most powerful government on Earth.

"I also helped preserve God's people for His greater purpose. The realisation of my dream far exceeded my expectation. God has for us, purposes that are more than we can imagine—more than our egos can take. He is the fulfiller of every dream He gives."

The primary reason for your dream is for you to solve a problem.

"The dream is not an ego booster. We all have been placed on Earth to solve a problem. My dream would, among other things, preserve the remnants of God's people (of which I was part) from extinction. It was also to preserve humanity from the ravages of famine.

"This is why He gave me the insight into how to preserve food—thus the first recorded evidence of food preservation. Through the God-given idea, I was able to initiate the building of giant state-of-the-art storage facilities capable of storing food for the next seven years of famine which I predicted as part of the dream Pharaoh had.

"As a result of this, the nation and surrounding countries were able to survive the harsh seven-year famine which preceded the previous years of abundance. As a bonus, I was also able to generate enough revenue from the sale of grain for the national treasury, thus making Egypt an economic powerhouse in the world—all because I held on to the dream and with God's strength saw its fulfilment.

"If there is one thing I would say in closing, it is this—for all the dreams you have and for what they're worth, do not think of abandoning them, for they will surely come to pass. Also remember that God is with you as you go through the difficult periods in the journey. And it always pays to adopt a life of integrity into every facet of your life, for this is what guarantees the fulfilment of those dreams."

With these words of encouragement, Joseph prays for us:

Dear Lord,

I am not asking you to relieve every pain experienced by this generation; I ask that you strengthen them to fulfil their purpose. Make your dream for their lives clear and plain in their minds, and give them the heart to keep running the race of life. Amen.

When Joseph finishes praying, he reaches out and grabs each of our hands and gives it a quick squeeze and a firm shake of encouragement. Then he departs from the track.

Wow! We feel encouraged.

Personal Prayer of Renewal

Lord, I thank you for your love and grace which is making a difference in my life. I thank you for assuring me of the dreams you have given me.

I ask for strength and courage to persevere in times of difficulties and circumstances beyond my control. Continue to stand beside me as I nurse the dream in my heart as a seed. That like a seed planted in the right soil, I will plant the seed in the soil of preparation and character building. Help me to stay calm when the storms of life rise; when situations threaten to abort the dreams You have given to me.

Help me understand that these circumstances are not there to destroy me, but rather to prepare me for the manifestation of Your glory about to be revealed. This I ask through your son, Jesus Christ my Lord. AMEN.

In Summary

This is what Joseph wants you to know about living today from his experience:

- Worthwhile dreams and visions come from God.
- A dream can only be fulfilled when it has God as its source.
- Your family and friends may not always agree with the dream, so they may not support it.

- Remember that although you may not receive your family's support, God is always with you on the journey.
- You will encounter many obstacles—they are there to promote you and not to harm you.
- The vision is usually for an appointed time. Between the revelation and its fulfilment is always a process.
- Obstacles also unearth abilities, skills, and talents that you did not notice you have.
- Your dream is not an ego booster. There are many people who will be blessed as a result of your obedience.
- The world is groaning and waiting anxiously for the manifestation of your dream.
- When successful, the dream will bring you from obscurity to prominence.
- Self-promotion will not get you there. Divine promotion will.
- You should not sell your birthright for a bowl of soup because of the power of the dream

Chapter Six: David The Shepherd-King

The next member of the cloud of witnesses perhaps more than anyone else, is the person we would most like to encourage us as we strive to live our lives today. For one thing, he is a great man by all standards since his life has had tremendous impact on the history of people in Israel and still continues right up to this day. There are people who regard him as the most successful ruler in the history of humanity.

The interesting thing about him is that he started off in life in the worst possible place to be. Indeed, one could say that he was way ahead of his time when he came into prominence. As we look on intently to see who is coming in to bring heavenly wisdom into our lives, he approaches us.

He is dressed as a king in colourful robes with a jewelled sword on his hip and a crown on his head, but at the same time carries himself as a great warrior—powerful and yet relaxed, alert, and poised for any situation.

We wonder what the greatest king of Israel will say to us. Will he talk about the various military campaigns he led during his reign? Will he share the loneliness he felt as he hid from King Saul or perhaps, he will share his amorous encounters with the beautiful woman which almost caused him his throne and kingship? Or perhaps, he will tell us about how he expanded Israel's territory, thus ushering in a golden age of stability and economic prosperity for God's people or how he felt when he wrote parts of the Bible which continue to encourage and lead people into intimate worship with God.

He is a man after God's own heart, so any word that falls from his lips will be priceless—worth more than the best stones in the world.

As he moves closer, we can see he is a man who has seen and experienced a lot in life—pain, grief, rejection, and even death; yet, he doesn't look bitter or hardened. His demeanour is open, and as he comes alongside us, he says, *"You can overcome the limitations people put on you to rise and become what God has ordained you to be."* This really sounds heavenly as he utters those words of wisdom. With those words, we feel we are in for an exciting run.

And in case you haven't noticed, the person we are referring to is David, the man who in spite of his hubris, is described as *"a man after God's own heart."* This must be one unique description of someone who started off on a challenging note. But as he rightly tells us, if he was able to overcome the obstacles placed on him by society and family, then we can also shrug off the stereotype and rise to be *"shepherd-kings."*

He may have been born centuries before many of us were born, and certainly the settings in his time are vastly different from our technologically advanced society. But the vital life lessons he learnt and wants to impart to us are still relevant and as contemporary today as they were back then—something that makes him well worth listening to.

When we think of David, we don't immediately think of limitations. Here is a man who achieved great success and made it to the top. He was a great warrior and a great king in Israel's history. Yet, there were many who never saw his potential as he amply explains.

"As a teenager, I certainly did not look like a warrior; neither did I look like king material. Perhaps, with the benefit of hindsight, this is the way I saw myself and so like the famous grasshopper mentality, so was I in the eyes of my family and those around me. I was an ordinary shepherd boy.

"The greatest battles in my teenage years were not necessarily the ones I fought against the lions and bears who came in to devour my father's flock which was under my care. The greatest battles I have had to face were the ones created by people and the society who tried to put limitations on me. And to prove this, here are a few examples of the limitations I had to deal with:

Jesse, my father did not think I had a king-potential.

"Do you often feel you are not appreciated for what you're worth? And that people do not think you have what it takes to rise to the level God has ordained you to be? Well, I had to face a similar situation.

"My father, Jesse, became excited when he learnt that Samuel, the prophet and God's anointed spokesman, was coming to anoint one of his sons as the next king of Israel after he had rejected Saul for disobeying Him. He probably must have discussed the prospect of having one of his boys crowned as the next king of Israel with my mother—comparing all of us and which one was most suitable.

"As the story unfolds, when Samuel arrived to perform the royal ceremony, my father and indeed, the man of God were quick to conclude that one of my older brothers would be a more suitable candidate to wear the crown. But they had the shock of their lives when God had other plans. None of the strong, macho men were eligible candidates for the highest office of the land. It is recorded in scriptures that:

When they arrived, Samuel saw Eliab and thought, "Surely the Lord's anointed stands here before the Lord." But the Lord said to Samuel, "Do not consider his appearance or his height for I have rejected him. The Lord does not look at the things man looks at. Man looks at the outward appearance but the Lord looks at the heart."
1 Samuel 16:6-7 (NIV)

"After running through all the eligible candidates, it became apparent that God was looking for someone outside the box. God's way of choosing people to execute an assignment is not what we think. This should offer a glimmer of hope to many of you out there. If society says you are unsuitable for the job simply because you are black, white, man, woman, short, tall, fat, and slim, remember you are valued in God's eyes. In cases like these, all you have to do is focus on what God has said about you, for that is what will get the job done.

"Having exhausted the entire Jesse family except me, it became clear I was the one God had chosen. I was in the pasture taking care of my father's livestock. Never did it cross my father's mind that I would be chosen to lead God's people. To some extent, I did not matter so far as the family was concerned. But that was when God decided to use the foolish things of the world to confound the wise so that all the glory would go to Him rather than men. Isn't that reassuring to know God values us for who we truly are even if our family doesn't; even if we are teenage shepherds?

So he asked Jesse, *"Are these all the sons you have?" "There is still the youngest,"* Jesse answered, *"but he is tending the sheep."* Samuel said, *"Send for him; we will not sit down until he arrives." So he sent and had him brought in. He was ruddy with a fine appearance and handsome features. Then the Lord said, "Rise and anoint him; he is the one."*

1 Samuel 16:11-13 (NIV)

"Similarly, your generation faces a lot of limitations and stereotyping placed on it by the society they live in. You have to realise that it is what God says about you that matters. What people and society have put on you is only artificial, man-made and can be overturned; primarily by not *'conforming any longer to the pattern of this world but be transformed by the renewing of your mind ...'* (Romans 12:2).

"You have what it takes to make a meaningful impact on your family, community, and nation. God in His infinite wisdom often uses the most unlikely people to do extraordinary things for His kingdom. Remember Paul, when he was Saul, persecuted the very thing he was born to defend? Remember earlier on, Gideon, the mighty man of valour? He wants to use you as you are."

My brothers did not think I had warrior potential.

"I had to endure similar rejection from my brothers. When Israel went into war with the Philistines, three of my brothers were enlisted in the army while I was left at home to continue with my chore—taking care of my father's livestock. So when my father sent me to find out how they were doing and also to bring back news of what was happening on the battlefield, I took the opportunity to acquaint myself with military warfare and how my country's army was doing. That was when I first caught a glimpse of the Philistine warrior, Goliath. He was quite a massive man, a fighter right from birth.

"With Goliath taunting the Israelite army in battle, I took on the challenge of facing the *'uncircumcised Philistine'* who at this time had defiled God's people. That is when the attacks and the discouragement came in—from my own brothers:

When Eliab, David's oldest brother heard him speaking with the men, he burned with anger at him and asked, "Why have you come down here? And with whom did you leave those few sheep in the desert? I know how conceited you are and how wicked your heart is; you came down only to watch the battle."
1 Samuel 17:28 (NIV)

"So far as my brothers were concerned, the battlefield was only suitable for the physically and mentally strong, and I wasn't any of that. But I was as strong as they were because I had experiences which qualified me to confront Goliath, contrary to what they had thought."

Back-of-the-desert Experience

"While I was largely unnoticed in my family, I was experiencing a brave, new world out there on the back side of the desert, mainly taking care of my father's livestock. I would later find out that those experiences were the training grounds for such occasions as the ones the Israelite army faced. It was almost as if I was being groomed precisely for this moment. It was time to put all the skills I had acquired with the lions and bears to practice as I later pointed out:

David said to Saul, "Let no one lose heart on account of this Philistine; your servant will go and fight him." Saul replied, "You are not able to go out against this Philistine and fight him; you are only a boy and he has been a fighting man from his youth."

But David said to Saul, "Your servant has been keeping his father's sheep. When a lion or a bear came and carried off a sheep from the flock, I went after it, struck it and rescued the sheep from its mouth. When it turned on me, I seized it by its hair, struck it and killed it. Your servant has killed both the lion and the bear; this uncircumcised Philistine will be like one of them because he has defied the armies of the living God ..."

1 Samuel 17:32-36 (NIV)

"Taking care of my father's flock became the fertile grounds to learn modern guerrilla warfare tactics which would come in handy in situations as the ones we were presented with.

"Many of you have experienced a lot of hardships as well as some training largely from the school of life. If you will see those experiences as the preparatory stage of greater things to come, it will put you in a unique position to tackle your Goliath head-on. But once again, there are those who would question your credentials and your combat readiness.

"From my experience, I would say ignore those brothers and draw strength from the source of all life who knows you and thus knows what your abilities and capabilities are to fulfil the challenge ahead of you."

Is There Not a Cause?

"The experience I went through taught me life's most important lesson: often there is a cause for everything that happens on Earth. And there are also seasons in which we come alive as solution carriers to the problems our society faces. Many years later, my son, Solomon, rightly pointed this out:

There is a time for everything and a season for every activity under heaven; a time to be born and a time to die, a time to plant and a time to uproot ...
Ecclesiastes 3:1-2 (NIV)

"The training I went through in the desert was going to come in handy at the right time as we now know. I certainly did not know there was going to come a time when I would be unleashed onto the world to bring deliverance to many people.

"There is a cause for everything you are experiencing right at this moment in your life. You are being prepared in the desert where nobody sees you for an opportune time which will come very soon. In your season of waiting, remember that society may ignore you; they may not even acknowledge your existence, let alone your presence, but just remember God is preparing you through these difficult times if you let Him, and also realise He is using these valley experiences to build you up into a mighty giant.

"Always remember that with God, all things work together for those He loves, which includes you, and also for those who are called according to his purpose, which again includes you!

"So, not only did the back-of-the-desert experience prepare me, but it also gave me a precedence to fall on which made all the difference as I defeated the great warrior, Goliath, with a stone and a sling. What a great story!

"My brothers may have seen me as nothing more than an errand boy, but I was really a man on a mission.

"King Saul did not think I had champion potential. When King Saul heard there was someone in the camp who was willing to fight Goliath, he sent for me. He was no doubt expecting a seasoned veteran to face the nine-feet-nine-inches tall Philistine warrior. Who walks in but a shepherd-boy saying *'Let no man's heart fail because of Him; your servant will go and fight with this Philistine.'*

"Saul's response reveals his scepticism. He said to me:

'You are not able to go against this Philistine to fight him; for you are a youth and he is a man of war from his youth.'

1 Samuel 17:32-33 (NIV)

"Saul definitely thought I wasn't champion material and that I wasn't up for the task.

"People will often think because of your age, upbringing, or background that you are not cut out for the top, although you are well able to, and I was, too, as I later proved. The secret once again is seeing yourself in the eyes of God.

"This may sound simple, but how many people have lost or missed the opportunity to become solution carriers simply because they did not see themselves in the right light—rather, they saw themselves as grasshoppers?

"I didn't allow Saul to hinder me with his low expectation or his bulky armour. I went out to face Goliath just as I was. It was not too much about wearing the best armour money could buy. I just went in as I was with God's strength backing me, and the rest as they say is history."

Goliath did not think I had even opponent potential.

"The worst insult for anyone is to be told he or she is incompetent or perhaps not fit enough to carry out a task. This is how I felt when Goliath saw me advancing towards him in battle.

"The huge Philistine took one look at me, a shepherd boy, and reacted negatively:

So the Philistine said to David, "Am I a dog that you come at me with sticks?" And the Philistine cursed David by his gods. "Come here," he said, "and I'll give your flesh to the birds of the air and the beast of the field."

1 Samuel 17:43-45 (NIV)

"Goliath despised me and believed I wasn't even worthy of a proper burial, and with those words, he attacked me.

"One can easily determine the calibre of a person by the amount of opposition it takes to discourage him or her. I faced great opposition. In fact, everyone told me I had no potential, but at the same time, I was able to:
- Go beyond my family (relational limitation)
- Go beyond King Saul (leadership limitation)
- Go beyond Goliath (Skills limitation)

"Indeed, I had to throw off the limitations other people placed on me and killed Goliath in the process. It was a great victory as well as vindication. Once again, God used me to prove the sceptics wrong. By defeating the Philistine, I also managed to remove the limitation on the armies of Israel as it empowered them to complete the victory by routing the Philistines' army.

"My personal victory turned into a victory for the entire nation of Israel. How about that for shrugging off the limitations society and the world at large puts on you?!

"My brothers and sisters, you can do it!"

This is almost as we imagined it to be and even more. We feel the gates of brass and iron opening right before our eyes. We have what it takes to reach the summit, to live the life God ordained for us. This has been the theme running through all the great men and women who have inspired us up to now. There is no way we can fail our generation. We are in a better position than we have been for generations to pass on a positive legacy to the next generation.

The stereotype our society has placed on us does not affect us in any way. It is God's word that has the final say in who we are and what we become. And so far, everything is pointing towards rising up and flying high, the flag of our liberator.

As we take in all he has said to us, we can't help but wonder how he was as a boy and how even he—a man after God's own heart who grew up to be a great king — had to start out with nothing but hope and potential and also with all the odds firmly stacked against him.

We are quickly snapped out of these reflective thoughts by his desire to share these final words of wisdom with us:

Limitations don't limit us unless we let them.

"My father, my brothers, and the king all thought I had no potential. But quite contrary to what they thought, I had the greatest potential of all: I had God-potential. My days of looking after my father's livestock proved to be a defining moment in my life as God used those periods to build into me qualities and character traits that would fit a king. In a nutshell, I had all the potential and more.

"When I was young, I was able to keep growing in spite of the negative reactions of others because of God's help. I never forgot the day Samuel anointed me. From that day on, the spirit of the Lord came upon me in power.

"Then I realised God could strengthen me to rise above the limitations life and others tried to put on me. My friends, He can also do that for you.

Don't try to be someone else when others impose limitations on you.

"When Saul realised I was going to fight Goliath, he tried to put his armour on me. In effect, he wanted me to attack the problem as he would. I tried the armour on only because he intimidated me, but it didn't fit. It is a big trap to try and do things prescribed by the world which is represented by popular culture.

"At that moment, I realised God didn't want a substitute Saul; He wanted me. God will never hold you accountable for gifts you don't have or responsibilities He hasn't given you. He wants you to be yourself.

When you rise above your limitations, you can help others do the same.

"You see, the day I faced Goliath, I only thought of defeating him. I never realised my victory would invariably become the victory of the entire nation. The moment Goliath fell, the army of Israel rose and took their rightful place.

"Their fear and intimidation were replaced by courage and aggressiveness. On that day, I learnt my greatest leadership lesson—*people follow the example of their leader.*

"The moment I accomplished more than anyone thought was possible, all hell broke loose as people were empowered to do the impossible, all because there was a sudden surge of confidence in people's ability to achieve whatever they dreamt or imagined."

Except the Lord builds, those who build labour in vain.

"It is often very easy for us to jump on a bandwagon or our little crusade bent on fulfilling what God has said.

Nothing can be further from the truth. When I was anointed as king, I still acknowledged Saul as the Lord's sovereign choice and so I did not manoeuvre or conspire to assert myself as king. I was prepared to wait for the appointed time before I took over the throne. I was prepared to leave everything into the hands of the one who had ordained me.

"When we receive any promise or prophecy from God, our responsibility is to watch as God performs His word in our lives. Premature actions often lead to the whole promises being missed.

"When I had the perfect opportunity to get rid of Saul, I still was not prepared to lay a finger or shed the blood of someone God still had chosen to govern His people. Allow God to establish you. He is the king-maker!"

Be at the right place at the right time.

"This is often echoed in your world most of the time, but it is true that being at the right place at the right time makes all the difference in bringing out the champion in you. Unfortunately, I cannot say with confidence that I wholeheartedly followed this generally accepted truth. In fact it is recorded in scripture that:

In the spring, at the time when kings go off to war, David sent Joab out with the king's men and the whole Israelite army. They destroyed the Ammonites and besieged Rabbah.

But David remained in Jerusalem. One evening, David got up from his bed and walked around on the roof of the palace. From the roof, he saw a woman bathing.

> *The woman was very beautiful and David sent someone to find out about her. The man said, 'Isn't this Bathsheba, the daughter of Eliam and the wife of Uriah, the Hittite?*
> *Then David sent messengers to get her. She came to him and he slept with her ...*
> 2 Samuel 11:1-4 (NIV)

"This is a classic example of being at the wrong place at the wrong time. At a time when I should have been with my troops, giving them moral and spiritual support, I was at home, and this led me to committing the most abominable act ever committed. It was the worst position to be in. I saw what I should not have seen and did something I shouldn't have done. And the consequences?

"I basically committed adultery by getting the beautiful and married Bathsheba into bed. To add to this, I also committed murder by instigating the death of Uriah, Bathsheba's husband, to make it look like he was killed in the line of duty—what a clever way to cover one's tracks.

"But as I later found out, nothing is hidden forever from God. I nearly lost everything God gave me had I not humbled myself. However, the 'love child' from the affair died.

"My children openly revolted against me, and the list goes on and on. All of this, as a result of being at the wrong place at the wrong time.

"Similarly, as the future of the next generation, it is important to learn the value of being in God in order to continue receiving nourishment to bear fruit:

"Remain in me and I will remain in you. No branch can bear fruits by itself; it must remain in the vine.

Neither can you bear fruits unless you remain in me.

I am the vine; you are the branches. If a man remains in me and I in him, he will bear much fruit; apart from me, you can do nothing."

John 15:4-5 (NIV)

"Just know where God wants you to be and stay there. And if you are not sure, call onto Him and He will answer you and show you great and mighty things you do not know (Jeremiah 33:3).

"He is the one who will lift you up. Remember that He is also a God of another chance. If He gave me a second chance, He will surely give you one."

And with those last words, David bows and makes his way out. How blessed we have been to receive such incredible words of encouragement from the man who has seen it all—from the back of the desert to being crowned king to being pursued by Saul to a one-night stand which results in an incredible internal and external conflict to becoming "the man after God's own heart."

And yet, he is so calm and measured in his demeanour, pouring his heart out to us as if we were his own children. But before he leaves us, he offers to pray for us:

Father, I thank you for the lives of these incredible men and women you have given me so I can encourage them. I pray that you open the eyes of their understanding to who they truly are in you.

Most importantly, I pray that you strengthen them as well as help them cast off any stereotype or limitations their families and society as a whole may have placed on them.

Let them see themselves the way you see them—as mighty men and women of valour who can do exploits through you who strengthens them. Let them also come to the realisation that the world is earnestly waiting for their manifestation. Only then will they be able to prove your good, perfect, and acceptable will for their lives.

I thank you in the name that is above all names, Jesus, our Saviour, and the son of the living God, AMEN.

In Summary

This is what David wants you to know about living today from his life experience:
- You can put off the limitations people and society have put on you to become all that God has created you to be.
- There are those who think you don't have the requisite skills to achieve what you've been called to achieve—it's God's call, not theirs.
- Limitations don't limit us unless we let them.
- Don't try to be someone else when others impose limitations on you.
- When you rise above your limitations, you can help others do the same.
- Be at the right place at the right time.
- Except the Lord builds, those who build labour in vain.

Chapter Seven: Nehemiah Owning a Cause

After listening to these great giants of the faith and receiving encouragement from them, we feel confident about the race ahead of us. For one thing, if these men who have weaknesses and failings just like us can inspire so much confidence as well as change the course of history, there is no doubt that, after such motivation and encouragement, we can also run with faith, confidence, and perseverance the race set before us.

What wisdom and perspective they have given us! So far, Gideon has taught us to discover the hero in us and use it to bring light to our generation. Joseph, on the other hand, has encouraged us not to abandon our dreams, since it is that which would bring purpose to our lives.

With such impartation from these heroes of faith, we wonder what is in store for us!

As we prepare for what is to come, the next hero approaches to speak to us. He looks like an official of some sort, wearing a gold chain around his neck, as a representation of his status. He also carries a small scroll. What could the scroll contain? Could it contain the assignments God has given to us? Or could it contain the judgments of an all-powerful Creator ready to be unleashed on humanity?

The man looks at us and senses our excitement at living our lives today with purpose and urgency. Like the writer of Hebrews, we are ready to run our race with perverance. As he turns to address us, he says the following:

"I'm Nehemiah. There are a lot of causes you can commit your life to; thereby channelling your passion and energy into it. These causes give you an opportunity to make a difference in your world.

"Contrary to popular culture, you do not ALWAYS need the voice of God or that special voice or inner conviction to figure out your purpose.

"The purpose, meaning, and fulfillment you seek is all around you, merely awaiting your recognition. This was what happened to me as recorded in the Bible.

"I was a cupbearer to King Artaxerxes of the great kingdom of Persia, enjoying all the privileges my position brought even though I was a Jew. Such was the importance of my position that I became what would be termed in modern politics as the king's trusted aide or personal advisor. To give you an example of my importance, I often had to taste all the food to prevent any harm to the king. I put my life on the line for the security and protection of the king, which brought us very close.

"You see, although I was a Hebrew working in the royal courts of Persia, I was mindful of my ancestral heritage. Despite the fact that I had become fully assimilated into the Persian culture, my heart was still with my people—the people of Israel. That is why, when I heard the news about the broken walls of Jerusalem, I did not hesitate to take action." This is how it is recorded in the Scriptures:

> *In the month of Kislev in the twentieth year, while I was in the citadel of Susa, Hanani, one of my brothers came from Judah with some other men and I questioned them about the Jewish remnants that survived the exile and also Jerusalem.*
>
> *They said to me, "Those who survived the exile and are back in the province are in great trouble and disgrace. The wall of Jerusalem is broken down and its gates have been burned with fire. When I heard these things, I sat down and wept ..."*
> Nehemiah 1:1-4 (NIV)

"Although I was enjoying the privileges my position brought, I was quickly brought to my knees by the news of what was happening to the remnants of my people who had returned from exile. It would have been much easier to turn a blind eye to what was happening in Jerusalem, but that was not the case. Their problem became my problem—more than enough reason why I wept when Hanani and the delegation from Judah broke the news to me.

"I know it is often difficult to motivate yourself; to find a vision or mission to commit your life to. This is what is happening to a lot of young men and women of your generation. However, I am here to encourage you that, contrary to what you have seen or heard, there are many noble causes you can commit yourself to. Look around your neighbourhood and community, and you will see a broken and dying world in desperate need of resurrection—a situation which needs urgent attention. And, like me, God is calling you to own the cause of rebuilding your world by being part of the solution if not the solution.

"The world you live in is the visible expression of a heavenly realm masterminded by a generous Creator and the Author of life. Out of His generous love, He created a visible world with a semblance to the heavenly realm. At the peak of everything He created, He made man in his image and likeness with the sole responsibility of managing this visible world, the earth domain which He created. The Bible expressly recalls:

Then God said: "Let us make man in our image and likeness and let them rule over the fish of the sea and the birds of the air, over the livestock, over all the earth and over all the creatures that moves along the ground."

So God created man in His image, in the image of God He created him; male and female He created them. God blessed them and said to them: "Be fruitful and increase (multiply), fill the earth and subdue it. Rule over the fish of the sea and the birds of the air and over every living creature that moves on the ground."

Genesis 1:26-28 (NIV)

"Not only was man created to manage the earth domain, he was also given the authority to fulfill this responsibility. Such was the uniqueness of the mandate and harmony that existed between the Creator and the created. The scriptures record that:

Now the Lord God had formed out of the ground all the beasts of the field and all the birds of the air. He brought them to the man to see what he would name them; and whatever the man called each living creature, that was its name. So the man gave names to all the livestock, the birds of the air and all the beast of the field.
Genesis 2:19-20

"It was the intention of God, the Creator, that this union would continue for eternity. Unfortunately, this otherwise perfect world was shattered when sin gained a foothold and eventually filled the earth, hence the world we live in. That is exactly what happened when my people disobeyed God, their Creator.

"What you see today is the exact consequence of what happened when sin, which is separation from our creator, came into the world. This is because part of the deal at creation was that man would live the rest of his life with God, his creator at the centre of everything he did. We were created in His image and likeness. This means man has God's DNA in him so that as long as we recognised this, we would live a blessed life for eternity. It was when we got separated from God that sin and everything that came about as a result entered the world.

"But what are some of the things we have inherited as a result of our separation from God? One thing we have inherited is a broken world in which there is no respect for humanity nor the boundaries that have been set for our benefit.

"So how significant was the wall we had rebuilt you may ask?

"The wall was an important structure for the people of Israel. For one thing, it served as a means of protection. It ensured that the territorial sovereignty of Israel as an independent nation was well safeguarded. This meant no external aggression against it could ever succeed because it was heavily secured.

"With the protection of its boundaries came the preservation of the Jewish culture and identity. The walls made it possible for the people to continue to practice their culture and maintain the identity they had known since the days of the Patriarchs —Abraham, Isaac, and Jacob.

"Consequently, with the breaking down and burning of the walls, it meant that Israel had become vulnerable to the neighbouring nations. Of much importance was what was going to happen to the Jewish culture and identity, especially considering they had just begun to reassert their identity following many decades in captivity. They were on the brink of losing their identity as God's chosen people. This is why I was ready to give up the royal privileges I enjoyed in order to become the solution. As far as I was concerned, this was far more important than the relative comfort the palace of Persia provided me.

"God wanted someone to open their eyes to what was happening to his visible expression and to take immediate action in restoring it to its original state. Likewise, you have been called by God to open your eyes to the state of your neighbourhoods and communities, and restore them.

"You are being summoned to help rebuild the walls that have been broken down and burnt. Contrary to what you may believe, there are many walls in your culture that need to be rebuilt."

The Wall of Righteousness

"Solomon, the wisest king to have ruled in Israel, once said that *'righteousness exalts a nation but sin is a reproach (disgrace) to any people'* (Proverbs 14:34). The truth is your generation grapples with unrighteousness; it has become second nature to them. As you strive for a better world, righteousness, which is right standing with our Creator, God, has been pushed away from everything you do—in business, family life, the education system, and government among other things.

"In some parts of the world, God and everything He stands for have been fiercely rejected, much to the detriment of those societies—especially when one considers that these same societies had been founded and modelled on sound Godly principles.

"We have seen the rise in recent years of the Pro-Choice movement around the world which advocates, among other things, for the rights of women to decide on whether to keep a fetus growing inside of them or to get rid of it through abortion. This is taking place at a time when we should be rebuilding the all-important wall of procreation and right family values. This wall will help reestablish our identity as the people of God. There are voices of the millions of children rising out from the earth asking us important questions about our decisions to get rid of them. What rights do we have to make such decisions? Who gave us the authority to play God?

"You are being called as an army of men and women to rise and put a stop to this abominable act and others like it. Will you respond and help rebuild this wall?

"The church, which is supposed to be the pillar and foundation of the truth and righteousness, has been relegated to the background. Significantly, as one would observe, the more righteousness is thrown out of the window, the more destructive the society becomes, and every evil intent of man thrives in such environments.

"This is why sexual immorality and perversion, false truths, unnatural love and relationships, wickedness, idolatry, hatred, and the lust of the flesh are so prevalent in our society. This generation may have been the most technologically-savvy, yet it is also the poorest generation morally and spiritually when it comes to righteousness and establishing the will of God, which by now far outweighs any information or technology.

"The Apostle Paul, many centuries ago, reiterated the importance of bringing righteousness back at the heart of humanity when he said that:

Creation waits in eager expectation for the manifestation of the sons of God.
Romans 8:19 (NIV)

"The young generation, just like mine, has groaned for a long time in earnest expectation. What is happening now will require men and women who are sensitive to what is going on around them and whose recognition as solution carriers is vital to the well-being of their generation. Until you rise to this challenge, the world will be in a perpetual state of decline. The future peace and stability of your society lies solely in your hands. Like my predecessor, Gideon, you are being called upon to uproot and tear down all unrighteousness and darkness which has gradually taken over this world and, in exchange, establish righteousness."

The Wall of Justice

"The world today is filled with so much injustice, one wonders whether this was the state at creation. From inequality in the redistribution of resources among communities to discrimination on the grounds of race, religion, sex, or creed, the list is endless. And if what we are witnessing is anything to go by, there is no indication this generation and the one to come will return to the 'good old fashioned' days of morals and principles which have been the backbone of human societies.

"People and nations covet the resources of other people and nations; they are prepared to do anything within their means and, in many cases, outside their means to get what they want, even when this means trampling over people. It is almost as if nothing has changed since Jesus came into the world and gave Himself up for a fair and better world. Do you remember the story of Naboth, Ahab, and Jezebel as recorded in the Bible? This is a classic example of the consequences when there is no justice.

"In this story, Naboth is unjustly murdered for refusing to give a piece of property, which had been in his family for centuries, to the king. At the instigation of the wicked queen, Jezebel, he is falsely accused of treason and then brutally murdered (1 Kings 21:1-29). Many men and women have been denied what is rightfully theirs. How unjust can that be?

"Many nations have been treated unjustly, causing them to lose what was rightfully theirs. The fragmentation of the world into developed and developing countries is another example of injustice. You are being called to bring restoration and rebuild the walls of justice, fairness, and equality; as God originally intended when He created man in His image and likeness with the express responsibility of managing the earth domain for Him."

The Wall of Identity

"If there is any one single most important wall that needs urgent restoration, it is, without a doubt, the *wall of identity*. The question of identity is the single biggest crisis facing young people today. Many are being led astray by the powerful force of consumerism represented by the media. In today's culture, people's self-worth is only measured by the amount or, in some cases, the quantity of material things one can amass.

"For many others, the strong desire to belong and be loved weighs heavily on their minds. Unfortunately, they do not receive the love and affirmation they crave for various reasons. While some parents may be unaware of what is going on in the minds of their children, others are sometimes too busy being parents to notice the internal struggle their children often go through.

"As a result, many young men and women find comfort, a sense of family, and belonging in the wrong crowd. This may not be ideal, but for the emerging generation, these crowds help establish their identity.

"You are being called to restore the true identity we were sealed with at creation. Humanity was created in no other image than the Creator Himself, so much so that He breathed His breath (Ruach) of life into us to become living beings. There is an urgent need to help deconstruct stereotyped identities placed on this generation almost entirely by society.

"As the Apostle Paul said, we are created to spread the message that:

'Everything is permissible for me but not everything is beneficial. Everything is permissible for me but I will not be mastered by anything.'
1 Corinthians 6:12 (NIV)

"We are called to encourage the emerging generation with this message to:

... offer our bodies as a living sacrifice, holy and pleasing (acceptable) to God – this is our spiritual act of worship.
Romans 12:1 (NIV)

"And that we should not:

...conform any longer to the pattern of this world; but be transformed by the renewing of your mind. Then you will be able to test and approve what God's will is – His good, pleasing and perfect will.
Romans 12:2 (NIV)

"However, in order for us to effectively carry out this task, we must first realise we have been placed in this unique position for a reason."

The Task of Rebuilding

"The news of the broken walls of Jerusalem hit me really hard, and I began to weep uncontrollably. The situation seemed hopeless, and I was helpless to do anything about it. In my grief, I turned to God, and He made me understand something—no problem is too big when you have help!

"Afterwards, I knew what I had to do—ask the king for help. In asking for help, I began to realise the rebuilding of the walls was not going to be the story of a single successful 'superstar,' rather, it would require many vision helpers; those who would understand the project's greater purpose and contribute in whatever way to help accomplish it. This was achieved when a record number of my people rallied around to complete the project in a record fifty-two days—a remarkable achievement. See what happens when you have people who are sold to the idea or vision!

"The walls were rebuilt because many people helped each other and worked together. The rebuilding process started with the help of the king, who agreed to send me to Jerusalem to accomplish the project (Nehemiah 2:1-9). When I got there, I again asked for help. My plea for help is recorded in the scriptures:

Then I said to them, "You see, the trouble we are in: Jerusalem lies in ruins and its gates have been burned with fire. Come, let us rebuild the walls of Jerusalem and we will no longer be in disgrace." I also told them about the gracious hand of my God upon me and what the king had said to me.

Nehemiah 2: 17-18 (NIV)

"The response I got from them was overwhelming, as they all agreed with a 'let us start rebuilding' battle cry."

At this stage, we have enjoyed how Nehemiah describes the way the people banded together, family by family, and worked for a remarkable fifty-two days with swords in one hand and trowels in the other, rebuilding the walls.

With the wisdom of someone who has rallied a group of people to do a work for God, similar to what we are being called to identify and work towards, Nehemiah shares with us the following:

We should ask others for help when the problem is bigger than us.

"The problem I faced was certainly bigger than I could imagine. Look at what I was up against:

I was geographically far from the problem when I learnt of it.

The people of Jerusalem had no materials to rebuild the walls.

The people had no will of their own to take on the huge project of rebuilding the walls. In fact, it looked like they had given up hope of ever rebuilding it.

Lastly, there was a great opposition to the rebuilding process from the neighbouring enemies who were represented by Sanballat, 'a certain Horonite,' and Tobiah, the Ammonite official. They represented the interest of those who were happy with the status quo; so they reacted angrily when they heard I had been given the mandate to rebuild and restore the walls of Jerusalem.

"Like me, there are those who are happy as long as you maintain the status quo; you continue to drift from one end to the other without any sense of purpose or vision.

"They are the Sanballats and Tobiases of this world, who would be deeply disturbed and angry because you have taken the initiative in committing to a worthwhile cause—the cause of God. It is recorded in the scripture that:

When Sanballat the Horonite and Tobiah, the Ammonite official, heard about this, they were very much disturbed that someone had come to promote the welfare of the Israelites.
Nehemiah 2:10 (NIV)

"Like me, when you face such problems, ones bigger than you can handle, it's not the time to get discouraged. Instead, it's time to get help."

We should ask others for help when the problem becomes personal.

"I did not allow the royal privileges of Persia to stop me from committing to a cause. The problem of Jerusalem became a personal problem for me. And as I indicated earlier on, you need to look around your surroundings, neighbourhood, and community for a cause to commit to.

"For me, the news was not some piece of foreign news. On the contrary, I became sad, but excited about the prospect of helping rebuild the walls.

We should ask others for help when we have shared the problem with God.

"The first thing I did when I heard about Jerusalem's condition was to take it to God in prayer. Too often, we try to carry the load of the problem all by ourselves, especially when He is the reason we are carrying the burden in the first place.

"Rather than carrying the load alone, He is the first person we should ask for help in any situation. Solomon reiterated the importance of asking God for guidance when he said:

Trust in the Lord with all your heart and lean not on your own understanding; in all your ways acknowledge Him and He will make your paths straight.
Proverbs 3:5-6 (NIV)

"The author of Hebrews also reiterates this point:
Let us therefore come boldly to the throne of grace that we may obtain mercy and find grace to help in the time of need.
Hebrews 4:16 (NIV)

We should ask others for help when we are willing to do our part.

"God wants to be our partner throughout life. Too often, we are tempted to carry the entire load ourselves or give everything to God and do nothing. God doesn't like either strategy. Sometimes, He moves before us and sometimes after us—but He doesn't move without us. Solomon wrote in Proverbs:

To man belongs the plans of the heart but from the Lord comes the reply of the tongue.

In his heart, a man plans his course but the Lord determines his steps. Proverbs 16:1,9 (NIV)

"Without God, we cannot move, and without us, God will not move. Just as I was willing to go halfway across the known world to do what I could, so should you."

We should ask others for help when we sense God's approval for the cause.

"When I prayed, I asked God to give me favour. As I obeyed Him, I increasingly sensed He had answered my request. When the king gave me permission to go back to Jerusalem and supplied me with letters and resources for the project, *'the king granted them to me according to the good hand of my God upon me'* (Nehemiah 2:8).

"When I stood before the people of Jerusalem, I encouraged them by telling them of the *'hand of my God which had been upon me'* (Nehemiah 2:18). Similarly, when opposition arose concerning the rebuilding of the wall, with confidence, I was able to say *'the God of heaven Himself will prosper us, therefore, we His servants will arise and build'* (Nehemiah 2:20).

"My increased awareness of God's blessing was a direct result of my continued obedience. *Never try to explain God until you've first obeyed.*"

We should ask others for help when people oppose us.

"Repeatedly, the people and I were faced with opposition. When I received permission and resources for the rebuilding project, the opposition, ably represented by Sanballat and Tobiah, was deeply disturbed (Nehemiah 2:9-10). Likewise, when the people declared their intention to rebuild the walls, they laughed at them and despised them. They became furious and indignant, and mocked us."

When Sanballat heard that we were building the walls, they became angry and was greatly incensed. He ridiculed the Jews ...
Nehemiah 4:1 (NIV)

"And when the people continued rebuilding the walls, the opposition conspired to attack them and create confusion.

"Motion always causes friction. Whenever God's people move forward, the enemy always increases his opposition, and that really turns up the heat. When others oppose us, it's not the time to give up. It's time to get help.

"Because we had God's backing, we were able to finish the rebuilding in a record fifty-two days. This is what we can achieve when we commit to a cause greater than us and when God is in our boat!"

Just when we are beginning to warm ourselves to what Nehemiah has been saying, we notice our time with him is very short, even though it feels like ages. His leadership is incredible, and there is so much we would like to learn from him. As we listen eagerly to his departing words, he shares some thoughts on his life:

There is so much around you to commit your life to.

"Look around you and what you see mirrors the heart of God for mankind. God is grieving for all the bloodshed, violence, and enmity tearing His creation apart. He is still looking for a remnant who will step up, feel His heartbeat, and commit their lives to the cause of saving mankind. You do not need to fast and pray for months to know the will of God— it is right there with you!"

It is not always easy to look for help.

"Even after I prayed and planned, I found it difficult to tell the king my heart's desire. Similarly, don't let insecurity, ego, or fear make you try to do it alone. In God's kingdom, there are people ready to help you at the right time and in the right way—people you don't even know."

Many times, you don't need a miracle, rather, you need each other.

"Many of the great people we hear of saw God provide for them miraculously. However, you don't need a miracle to do something miraculous. God has already provided all you need. We needed to work together. Without the leadership I provided, the people would have remained in ruins. My friends, you can run the race; your generation is counting on you! But also remember you cannot run alone."

With those words, Nehemiah makes his way out as we ponder what he's just told us. To think of the world looking up to us for a turnaround in our lives is an overstatement. Is he really saying there are a lot of worthwhile causes we can commit to without divine inspiration? This is very strange and goes against the grain of popular opinion and culture. Just as we chew on those words of encouragement, he turns around to pray for us:

Thank you, Father, for the lives of these great young men and women. I pray you will open their eyes of understanding to your cries and heartbeat, that they will begin to see the dysfunction in the world. I also ask that, as they see these destructions, they would be stirred to help rebuild the many walls broken and burnt.

Give them the courage, vision, and resources as well as vision helpers who will help them address the situation. In your mighty name I pray with much thanksgiving. AMEN

As he finally makes his way out, not only are we confident about the future, but we also understand we are not meant to live life by ourselves. This is such a great boost to us.

In Summary

This is what Nehemiah wants you to know about living today from his life experience:

- You have been called to rebuild the broken walls of righteousness, identity, and justice. Don't worry, because you have what it takes.
- Many times, you don't need to pray in order to discover a worthwhile mission to commit to. They are all around you.
- In the rebuilding process, you often need to ask for help from God and from people.
- You often need people who are dedicated to the task. That is all you need.
- God who knows you and your assignment will provide the resources you need to complete the task He gives you.

Chapter Eight:
Esther
You Were Born for Such a Time as This

What an incredible journey we've been on these past few chapters; it seems like we have been on this journey all of our lives. We have received Godly wisdom and encouragement from these incredible people, whose lives have helped shape the destinies of many people and cultures.

The question left on our minds throughout the journey so far has been: Where were all these men and women when we began our course of living life to the fullest? Surely, many of us would have been in a better place if we had had these people alongside us on our journey.

It certainly would have made life much easier for Tim, Sarah, and Jenny who still need guidance and encouragement from this great cloud of witnesses who have been there, seen it, and done it.

Perhaps, if there was ever a time for us to receive such inspiration from these people, it is now. The world may have succeeded in dishing out its brand of life and success to us for a long time, but we are on a mission to recover and restore everything the enemy, symbolised often by the world's systems, has stolen from us. And the good thing about it is that we are not alone. We have Gideon, Deborah, David, and Nehemiah whose invaluable support has equipped us with the confidence we need to live purposeful lives today.

Just as we pondered what we've listened to so far and the calibre of men and women who have come out to support us, our next hero of the faith approaches us; a woman elegantly dressed.

We do not know who she is. However, we are certain that, like all the other great people before her, we are going to receive an incredible wealth of wisdom and encouragement.

Her clothes are vibrantly coloured and appear to be made of the finest cloth available perhaps of the finest silk known at the time of her existence, and certainly of today. She is wearing gold jewellery and a crown dotted with precious gems. Her grace and demeanour lead us to believe she must be royalty—perhaps a queen or a member of a royal household.

As she gets closer, we notice she is a mature woman, breathtakingly beautiful. As she draws nearer, she seems to glide towards us. Then she begins to speak to us: "I have to tell you something important," she says. "God has a place for you. I also want you to know that you are not an accident. Rather, you have been born for such a time as this. Don't ever forget this. I know your society has made you feel worthless and insignificant, but I can assure you today that your life is about to take a new turn for the better."

Her voice is gentle, but strong and pleasing to the ear. We wonder who this elegant woman is. As we look intently in her direction, she simply says: "I am Esther."

If there was ever a person with a strong sense of purpose, place, and destiny, it is Esther. We remember her famous "If I perish I perish ..." statement and are quickly drawn to her, expecting to receive strong words of encouragement. This is a woman who was able to put her life on the line for her people. Surely, she has something to say to us that is worth listening to.

You see, for many of her years, she did not realise God had a special place for her to serve Him. Her story reminds us that we all have a special place to serve God by serving our own generation; that the world is not going to be whole, peaceful, and "perfect" until you and I have been able to recognise our calling and risen to it. This is what Esther seems to be telling us through her story. She continues...

"For much of my life, I felt out of place. My parents died when I was young, which made me an orphan at an early age. I was later adopted by my Uncle Mordecai. There were times I felt out of place in his home. As I grew up in a strange country with different customs and culture, I again felt out of place. And being a little girl brought to the king's court was also out of place. To say that I was an underdog would have been the understatement of all time.

"I lived during a time when the Jews had been taken captive from their homeland and exiled in Persia. Like my fellow brothers and sisters, I suffered many hardships, but that, in turn, opened the door to a rare opportunity when things started to change.

"Like me, you may have gone through rejection, hardship, and frustration. This has even led you to question why you were born. This is what the world wants you to believe. But know for sure that, like me, your life is about to take a turn for the better. There is a rare opportunity about to open for you—do not throw in the towel yet. It is still too early to do that.

"When King Ahasuerus of Persia, who was by far the wealthiest person in the known world, wanted a new queen because the previous one, Vashti, had misbehaved, this was the opportunity that brought me into the limelight. Her misbehaviour was seen as an open revolt against the king, but the consequences of her action went far beyond the royal courts.

"Since she was the '*mother*' of the kingdom and thus a shining example to the women in the land, her conduct would have given the entire female population of the land the 'license' to disobey their husbands and fathers—something the king was not prepared to tolerate in his wealthy kingdom, hence her immediate dethronement.

"In his search for Vashti's replacement, all of the most beautiful, young, unmarried women in the land were brought together and paraded before the king. And to do this, they had to undergo an intensive twelve months of beauty therapy and pampering before they could be paraded before the king. It is recorded in the Bible that:

Before a girl's turn came to go in to King Xerxes, she had to complete twelve months of beauty treatments prescribed for the women, six months with oil and myrrh and six with perfumes and cosmetics.
And this is how she would go to the king; anything she wanted was given her to take with her from the harem to the king's palace.
Esther 2:12-13 (NIV)

"Among the women who went through the beauty programme was yours truly, even though I was Jewish—a fact I did not share with anybody. After going through the programme successfully, to my delight and to the delight of my Uncle Mordecai, I was chosen by Ahasuerus to be the queen—what an honour to serve this great kingdom.

"At the same time, it was a huge responsibility on my shoulders, particularly for someone who had struggled to fit in with the excess baggage of being an orphan at a young age and also finding myself in a foreign country. This, for me, was the turning point in my life—a fact that was going to open my eyes to the real reason I was born.

"For a moment, it looked like my life was destined for a happy, storybook ending reminiscent of many Hollywood fairy tales. But then things took a turn for the worst when the very existence of my people was threatened by one of the king's officials. This was when I realised that I had been born, placed in the palace, not so that I could enjoy the comforts and luxuries of Persia, but rather for this specific reason. In other words, I had been born for such a time as this period.

"Haman, one of the king's trusted aides, plotted to exterminate the entire Jewish race because of my uncle's refusal to bow down to him. Having been recently honoured by the king for his exemplary leadership in the kingdom, Haman took his newfound authority too far, transforming himself into a demigod overnight. Scripture records that:

> *After these events, King Xerxes honoured Haman son of Hammedatha, the Agagite, elevating him and giving him a seat of honour higher than that of all the other nobles.*
>
> *All the royal officials at the king's gate knelt down and paid honour to Haman, for the king had commanded this concerning him. But Mordecai would not kneel down or pay him honour.*
> Esther 3:1-2 (NIV)

"When Mordecai discovered the plan to exterminate the Jews, he sought my help. To save our people, Mordecai wanted me to appeal to the king. Now, why would Haman want to exterminate my people? And why would I be the saviour of my people? After all, I am for all intents and purposes still the orphan girl who, not long ago, struggled to fit into the society. How can I suddenly be the saviour of my people? These were exactly the thoughts that went through my mind when I received the SOS message from Uncle Mordecai.

"It was during this season that threatened the existence of my people that I came into my own. It was the time I became a woman and realised my divine assignment—to deliver the Jews from Haman's evil plans.

"You see, many times we seem to be at a loss as to what our purposes are.

"Certainly in this generation, which often boasts of tremendous advancement in technology and things that make life easier, there is also a silent cry in the hearts of men and women for fulfilment and purpose. Many have a lot of education, but no purpose. Thus, it is no wonder that many people are doing all the right things according to the world's standards, but are still struggling to find that sense of significance.

"You have been born for such a time as this, although it may not seem like it at the moment. You will, like me, come into your own when the time is right. Do not allow society to tell you otherwise."

Finding Your Place

"Have there been times when you felt you weren't where you belonged? People often feel that way. We often lack close relationships with others. On other occasions, we question our ability to do the job required of us. Or we feel that, as a result of all the frustrations and difficult times we've been through, we do not have what it takes to move on in life. It is almost as if we are stuck with no way out.

"During these periods, we often feel out of place. We fear that we will never be able to amount to anything. I understand! This was exactly how I felt during those soul-searching periods. You may not have been uprooted from your culture and from your people. In fact, you may have been brought up in exactly the same place where you were born, but the dynamics of the society and the world at large have reduced your worth to that of anything other than successful, important, and ambitious.

"My answer to this is you have been born for a reason. Perhaps, like me, you may have been orphaned at an early age. This does not determine your self-worth. Your moments of fulfilment are just around the corner awaiting your recognition—albeit at the right time as ordained by the One who created and formed you."

By now, we are held spellbound by all this incredible wealth of wisdom and courage. As we listen intently, Esther encourages us with these words: "*No place is out of place when you are in God's place.*" Then she continues her story

"Mordecai's request for the salvation of the Jewish people was to unveil me into my destiny, but this was not a small request to make. In order for me to make a difference for my people required great courage and sacrifice. This was made evident when I had to make an approach to the king at a very difficult time.

"At the time, if anyone who had not been summoned by the king appeared before him, they would be executed. So, for thirty days, I had not been called to go before the king. If I went to him on my own, I would be risking my life. With the benefit of hindsight, I believed this was primarily because I did not yet understand that God had uniquely placed me where He wanted me in order to accomplish His will.

"As a result of this, I hesitated initially.

When Esther's words were reported to Mordecai, he sent back this answer: "Do not think that because you are in the king's house you alone of all the Jews will escape. For if you remain silent at this time, relief and deliverance for the Jews will arise from another place, but you and your father's family will perish. And who knows but that you have come to the royal position for such a time as this?"

Esther 4:12-14 (NIV)

"Mordecai, as a result of this rallying cry, reminded me of the whole purpose for my life. It was a light bulb moment as far as I was concerned. I realised that I had been born for a time such as this. My entire life culminated in this moment when I had to use my position to bring about the reversal of the fortunes of God's people.

"Looking back on it today, I am so privileged to have been the instrument God used to bring about this change in the fortunes of His people. It was not only the people I helped deliver, but more importantly, my own life was also at stake, as Mordecai rightly pointed out. The rest, as they say, is history.

"In the same way, your life's worth is waiting for the God-moment to happen. While it is being set out, remember you are not a failure. All the anxieties and frustrations are part of the overall preparation for the assignment. It may not look and sound like it at the moment, but things are being prepared for your good because you are loved and highly valued by God. He has called you according to His purpose.

"Now this is definitely something we should be happy about. For Sarah, Tim, and the many young men and women of the emerging generation, my encouragement to you is that you are in the overall plans of God. Society may forsake you, your family at some point may forsake you, but God hasn't. He's got you firmly in your hands.

"Mordecai's words changed the way I felt about myself. For the first time, I realised that God had a place for me. My initial hesitation was replaced by direction and determination. My questions and low self-worth were replaced by newfound convictions. I was ready to take action. This was my immediate response to discovering my purpose:

Then Esther sent this reply to Mordecai: "Go, gather together all the Jews who are in Susa and fast for me. Do not eat or drink for three days, nights or days.

I and my maids will fast as you do. When this is done, I will go to the king even though it is against the law. And if I perish, I perish."
Esther 4:15-16 (NIV emphasis added)

"I immediately realised my privileges as a queen were not just for my pleasure, but that I had been put in the palace for a purpose.

"Thus, courage and initiative come when you understand your purpose in life. What I experienced brings to mind the famous words of one of the greatest men who lived in the twentieth century, Winston Churchill:

"In every age, there comes a time when a leader must come forward to meet the needs of the hour. Therefore, there is no potential leader who does not have an opportunity to make a positive difference in society. Tragically, there are times when a leader does not rise to the hour."

"God not only has a place for us, He has placed us where He needs us. The decision is ours as to whether we will do what we can where we are."

Esther's story is a great source of encouragement to us. It is reassuring to know that God is always with us, and to know that, no matter where we are in life, we can be used by God. Esther isn't done yet—well, at least not quite. She gives us her final words of wisdom:

For a period of time, you may not know or if you know, understand the purposes and planning of God for your life.

"This was how I felt during the early days of my life. If you are in a season of life where you don't understand God's plans, take heart. Just because you don't understand God's plan doesn't mean there is no plan or that God doesn't care. Have faith and remain obedient to Him. Again, do not listen to what society says to you. Often their opinion of who you are is not the same as God's. Instead, get to know the Creator who formed you and who has a blueprint for your life."

When you realise God's purpose for your life, you often feel empowered.

"You see, when Mordecai explained to me that I was made queen because God wanted to use me and my position to bring about the redemption of the Jewish people, I felt valued and important—to be used as the instrument of God for His will to be accomplished. This, in turn, steeled my resolve.

"Similarly, when the time comes for you to recognise the call of God on your life, it will fire you into action—sometimes in the face of opposition or danger. When I approached the king, presenting my concerns to him about what Haman had plotted to do, I succeeded not only in realising the sovereign will of God, but also in exposing who Haman really was. This led to his own execution in the dungeon he had prepared for my people."

Taking risk is easier when you know God is in control.

"When I told Uncle Mordecai, '*If I perish, I perish,*' I was not trying to be fatalistic. Rather, I was trying to put my life into God's hands. I was, in effect, saying that, although it was not the right time to approach the king, the God I have known from birth is one who is above earthly principalities, kingdoms, and thrones, so He is the one who will take care of me and sort this issue out, knowing very well that death is something that can be faced with confidence when you trust God."

With those words, she prepares to depart from our presence, having delivered such inspiring and courageous words, often full of despair. If there is anything we can glean from what Esther has shared with us, it is this: we are all held in high regard by God. This offers us hope, particularly in a world that is often cruel and unsympathetic.

But before she leaves, Esther gives us one last piece of encouragement in the form of a prayer:

Dear Father,
I thank you very much for these men and women. I have no doubt in my mind that, having heard from these great men and women whom you have used to change the destinies of many people, they will be equipped to run the race you have set before them, knowing full well that you are there for them.

I pray for those who at some point in the future, or right now, are wondering whether there is anything meaningful about life and that you gradually open their eyes to the enormous potential you've placed in them. That not only will they realise this, but will, through your divine inspiration, be able to harness what you've given them to help create a better world for themselves and for those around them.

May they find significance and a sense of fulfilment in you rather than what the world tells them. This I ask in the name of our Lord and Saviour, Jesus Christ. Amen

In Summary

This is what Esther wants you to know about living today from her life experience:
- For a period of time, you may not know or understand the purposes and planning of God for your life. It doesn't mean God is not in control.
- When you realise God's purpose for your life, you often feel empowered.
- Taking risks is easier when you know God is in control.

Chapter Nine: Jabez Changing Destinies One Prayer at a Time

For someone whose life story occupies just a few lines in a book, you would wonder whether or not he had a significant life. Why would an account of his life fill just a few lines of a book?

Our traditional thinking leads us to believe it is only those who have lived lives of significance who fill pages of books and scriptures. In most cases, their stories stretch through chapters, and some cannot be contained in a single document.

So, how can someone's life story occupy so few lines?

This is where the next hero of the faith, the next member in the cloud of witnesses, comes in. Unlike all the other men and women who have spoken and shared their stories, there is nothing significant we can identify with him. He is not a great king like David, whom we have read about. Neither is he a great figure like the others we have come to associate with, particularly those who have captured the hearts of people by their simple, yet extraordinary lives.

Nonetheless, he is qualified to bring encouragement and wisdom into our lives. We wonder who this person is.

As he makes his way towards us, we do not immediately notice anything peculiar about him except he has an incredible sense of achievement about him. Like all the great men and women, he's faced many challenges. The odds have been firmly stacked against him, and yet, somehow, his demeanour shows someone who has overcome all of them.

And such is his level of personal achievement that he's got something to offer us. The suspense at this moment is at an all-time high when he eventually begins to speak...

"I'm Jabez, and I'm here to tell you that, despite the odds stacked against you, there is still light at the end of the tunnel. It is often not over until God says so. I know my appearance does not give any indication of what I have been able to do through God. Therefore, before you dismiss me, hear me out ...

"I was the head of a family in Judah, as is mentioned in 1 Chronicles 4:9. In addition to this, I was named after an unidentified town (Jabez) where scribes, who were my descendants, carried on serving God. What I have just mentioned may sound insignificant compared to the great achievements by the great men and women who have come before me.

"But I want also to remind you this was not the case when I was first born. My life was a far cry from the one I have just described to you."

Against the Odds

"When I was born, nobody ever predicted my life would turn out the way it did. In fact, all the evidence pointed to a life of average and defeat. I doubted I would ever have the opportunity to speak and bring encouragement to you.

"I particularly identify with Sarah whom you met earlier, and it seems, like me, she had been relegated to the scrap heap of life. My encouragement is that there is light at the end of the tunnel. Here are a few factors I had to come to terms with:

My name was a name of defeat.

"For some reason, my mother went through a lot of hardship when she was pregnant with me. Perhaps, it may have been that my biological father did not want anything to do with me. So, he left before I was born, leaving my mother with the responsibility of bringing me up, shaping my worldview, and picking up the pieces. This is reflected in the name I was given.

"The name Jabez in the Hebrew language means *'to grieve.'* Scripture records the circumstances surrounding my birth as follows:

Jabez was more honourable than his brothers. His mother had named him Jabez saying, "I gave birth to him in pain."

Chronicles 4:9 (NIV)

"The pressure and hardship my mother went through was reflected in the name she gave me and represented the life I was about to embark on. To sum it up perfectly, my life was nothing but hopelessness, lack of vision and direction.

Coupled with the name was the environment I was going to grow up in.

"I was looked down upon, and nobody expected me to do anything meaningful with my life. In short, everything about me and around me was set for a life of mediocrity and failure. It was pretty much the end of the dark tunnel for me. But that is precisely when the light began to shine.

"The light began to shine for me, giving me a better outlook when I discovered a secret—*prayer and the confession of faith.*

"I learnt that, through these two vital ingredients, I could nurse my way back to fruitfulness, effectiveness, and productivity; that my life would take on a whole new meaning if I would put these principles into my daily life.

"Scripture records exactly how I embraced these principles, making them my friends:

Jabez cried out to the God of Israel, "Oh that you would bless me and enlarge my territory! Let your hand be with me and keep me from harm so that I will be free from pain," and God granted his request.

1 Chronicles 4:9-10 (NIV)

"I was determined to shake off the negative stereotype I had been associated with. And God granted my request for three main things. These were:

Blessing for a new life

"I did recognise at some point in my life that the blessings of God were not just for a privileged few. Rather, it's always been on His mind to bless every man and woman. Indeed, at the beginning of creation, He blessed our ancestors, Adam and Eve, giving them dominion over everything He had created (Genesis 1: 26-28).

"And as a direct descendant of Abraham, the man who believed God and was accounted to Him as righteousness, I also became aware that the promise of divine blessings were not just for him and his family, but rather for everyone who would believe in God. In fact, I remember very well what God told Abraham when He said:

I will make you a great nation; I will bless you and make your name great. And you shall be a blessing. I will bless those who bless you, and I will curse him who curses you; and in you all the families of the earth shall be blessed.

Genesis 12:2-3 (NKJV, emphasis added)

"With this knowledge in mind, I was determined to claim what was rightfully mine and was not disappointed. God granted my request! This should encourage you to know that, when you make a petition that lines up with His promises, He answers!

"You will be interested to know that He's still interested in blessing people in your post-modern world as He was back then. As far as He's concerned, nothing has changed.

Enlarge my territory

"Having understood what my inheritance was, I also learnt an important truth: that God had given us opportunities to do extraordinary things; things beyond our wildest imaginations. I learnt that we can rightfully expand our sphere of influence beyond what our minds can ever imagine. Besides, it was His original intention at creation to give us dominion and authority to manage the earth-domain on His behalf. I read from scriptures one of the commands God had given to my people about not holding back and expanding our territory:

Enlarge the place of your tent; stretch your tent curtains wide. Do not hold back; lengthen your cords, strengthen your stakes.

For you will spread out to the right and to the left; your descendants will dispossess nations and settle in their desolate cities.

Isaiah 54:2-3 (NIV)

"Though difficult it seemed, partly because I did not know anything else apart from a life of mediocrity, I was able to discover basic but vital truths He had already laid down at creation. I was able to use this to the best of my ability, and that made all the difference.

Divine protection and security

"If I was to step into and enjoy all the blessings God had for me, I needed relative peace and security from Him. Since He was the one providing the blessings, I also found that He gave his children peace and protection from their enemies, those who opposed everything He stood for. So I was not afraid to ask for His divine protection since it was the only thing that could last.

"Another thing I learnt was that God grants the prayers of those who diligently call for His help. This, I can tell you because I am a living proof!"

What an incredible story. The fact that someone can change his outlook on life by petitioning God to do something about his situation is liberating to say the least. And, sure enough, God answers! As Jabez has shown, He grants deliverance from physical and spiritual destruction to all who call. He granted his request. He will do the same for you!

"You can also change the script of your life by rewriting it through the medium of prayer just like I have done. Remember that you just cannot go from having an average and mediocre life to becoming *'more honourable than his brothers'* (1 Chronicles 4: 6) just by existing and getting by. You should be prepared to change your worldview through prayer.

"We were all destined for greatness. That is how we were created to function; as people of extraordinary power. This is something I had to learn at later stages in my life when there was no hope. This is why, like me, you can also change the life you are currently living. You can have a life full of promise and fulfilment. But how, you ask?

"By simply adopting what I did, which I shared earlier. Prayer provides you with the formula for knocking on the doors of heaven for answers."

So, there you have it! Through the power of prayer (talking to God about everything and anything), you can rewrite the pages of your life; about how you want it to be and most importantly, the way He destined it to be!

This is a sure word of encouragement to us—that as we run with perseverance the race of life set before us, we can actually rewrite the pages of our lives through prayer and the confession of our faith. But what should we confess?

Jabez judges from our expression that we have something on our minds. So he proceeds to answer us:

Confess what the creator of your life has said about you.

"I am aware there are many people who do not know what has been said about them. It is because they have not bothered to find out. For others, the dynamics of modern life are so pressing that they often wonder whether or not there is anything meaningful or purposeful about life.

"To such people, I would say there are a lot of things said about them, their lives, and how things are going to turn out for them that there is not enough space and time to say all of it.

"But I can mention a few things already written about you in the Book of Life—the Bible:

Life of fruitfulness and dominion:

So God created man (you) in his own image, in the image of God He created him; male and female He created them.

God blessed them and said to them 'Be fruitful and increase in number; fill the earth and subdue it, Rule over the fish of the sea and the birds of the air and over every living creature that moves on the ground.'
Genesis 1: 27-28 (NIV)

The blessing of the Lord makes one rich and he adds no sorrow with it.   Proverbs 10:22 (NKJV)

Life of purpose:

Before I formed you in the womb I knew you. Before you were born I set you apart. I appointed you as a prophet to the nations.
Jeremiah 1:4-5, (NIV)

'For I know the plans I have for you,' declares the Lord, 'plans to prosper you and not to harm you, plans to give you hope and a future.'
Jeremiah 29:11 (NIV)

"If you have ever doubted your ability to live a fulfilled life, I am a living proof that you can by recognising the tools you have; *prayer and the power of confessing God's will over you.* And sure enough, when you pray and confess, He will grant your request."

With these words, Jabez gives us a firm squeeze on the shoulder and a handshake, making his way out, immediately to be followed by some physically challenged men who are eager to speak to us. As Jabez makes his way, we realise we have many questions to ask him, but we do not have enough time to do so.

In Summary

This is what Jabez wants you to know about living today from his experience:
- You can rewrite your life's story no matter how dark it may seem. He is a living proof of this.
- In changing your script, it often pays to find out what has been said about you. There is something decreed from eternity about you.
- There are two vital tools for your transformation: *prayer and the power of confession.* Prayer knocks on the doors of

heaven for answers, and the right confession brings you into agreement with what has been said about you.
- Jabez prayed for three things: blessing for a new life, to enlarge his territory, and divine protection and security.

Chapter Ten: The Four Lepers Taking Risk Is Not Always About You

There are times in life when the unexpected becomes the only alternative to what is considered normal. These are often exceptional times we come to accept for the purpose of progress and development. However, there are also times when what we experience becomes extraordinary if not unconventional.

It is often the case during these uncertain times that we wonder whether there is any moral in what we see, hear, and experience.

So far, we have been greatly encouraged by such great men and women whose courage, faith, and obedience to heavenly vision helped change the destinies of many lives. Their courage and willingness to submit to the sovereign authority of God have served as boosters for us as we strive to run the race of life set before us. Suddenly, there is a strong sense of confidence that we are not alone on this journey and that often, we have these visionaries and leaders cheering us on, which makes it even easier to run with perseverance.

Somehow, we have the confidence to believe that if, these men and women with weaknesses like we have, were able to achieve such great things, we are inspired to know that we can do much greater things as we follow in their footsteps. Again, we are encouraged by this truth.

Sometimes, in our bid to rise up to our calling, we often encounter people, circumstances, and situations we never anticipate will be the source of such great encouragement.

Donkeys have been used to bring life-changing messages and direction, restoring an entire nation. Devastating and unlikely situations have been used as the medium for great visions and victory during the course of human history. But nothing has really prepared us for what we are about to experience.

We are very excited about the next "giant" who will come and encourage us. What we have not realised is these men are not what you would expect—more so to encourage us.

Enter four leprous men who approach us. As they make their way to address and encourage us, we wonder if there has been a mistake. We are expecting mighty heroes, great military men, and powerful leaders; not four physically impaired men. Of all the varieties of the human species, the last group you would expect to provide us with encouragement is a bunch of invalids with self-confidence issues.

What could they possibly tell us that would inspire, encourage, and motivate us to run our race? What nuggets of wisdom have they got to offer us? We do not share the same struggles to qualify them giving us encouragement.

After all, they are invalids who are perceived to be the dregs of society. They drain our societies rather than add value to them. So what can such men offer us?

These thoughts produce mixed feelings of cynicism, but also of great excitement depending on the way one looks at it.

As we embark on this short journey of self-absorption, full of unanswered questions, one of the lepers begins to speak: *"Taking risks in life is not always about you. There are generations of men and women who are directly and indirectly released to fulfil their destinies.* Don't ever forget this."

These words shock us. And for once, we are almost hypnotised by such wisdom coming from the leprous. This, without a doubt, is one of those moments when the only way to get through to humanity as has happened in the past is to use the *"foolish things of the world"* to confound people with a vital message. To hear such nuggets of wisdom from unlikely sources is unconventional to say the least. It makes us want to know more. And so, we get more doses of this great "medicine" for our souls!

"Your fear of the unknown," they continue, "is stopping you from taking risks. This is such an essential element of human existence. Guess what happens when you don't step out? You paralyse other people from accessing what is rightfully theirs.

"Your action in getting out of your comfort zone automatically frees other people to soar like eagles—something they have been born to do. We are living examples of this.

"You see, we never knew we were the solution to a situation we had been part of until we decided reluctantly to take a risk into the unknown. That was when everything changed—stability was restored, and many generations lived to change the destinies of other generations and nations—all thanks to the power of risk-taking."

But what type of risk can physically-impaired men take? They are limited, so what could they possibly do? Their comfort zone is just to sit and beg. As we ponder on these soul-searching questions, one of them begins to speak:

The general circumstances of life often require risk-taking.

"When we are presented with dire circumstances, the answer is not in our resigning to allow the situation to take its course. Rather, it is the time we take steps to address the issue. And these steps are not business as usual. They require radical decisions that take us out of our comfort zones. And as is often the case, the initial reaction is that of fear and intimidation, but when we persist to the end, it turns out to be the best decision we have ever made.

"The period during which we took our risk was the most horrific we have ever known as a people. Scripture records that:

There was a great famine in the city; the siege lasted so long that a donkey's head sold for eighty shekels of silver and a quarter of a cab of seed pods for five shekels
2 Kings 6:25 (NIV)

"Such was the severity of the famine in the land, the people were reduced to a life of cannibalism:

As the king was passing by on the wall, a woman cried to him, "Help me, my lord and king." The king replied, "If the Lord does not help you, where can I get help for you?" Then he asked her, "What is the matter?"
She answered, "This woman said to me, 'Give up your son so we may eat him today and tomorrow, we will eat my son.' So we cooked my son and ate him. The next day, I said to her, 'Give up your son so we may eat him but she had hidden him"
2 Kings 6:26-29 (NIV)

"The general atmosphere was that of hopelessness, desperation, and abandonment which required radical, out-of-the box decisions to help rectify it.

"Often in life, you need radical, out-of-the-box thinking and decisions to help you rise from the challenging circumstances familiar to us. These out-of-the-box decisions are the ones that restore generations from the brink of moral and spiritual decadence. Therefore you must be prepared to make radical decisions when you are not happy where you are in life or with what you see around you. Taking these steps will help you liberate other people from similar situations. You cannot afford to fail the generation after you.

Being part of the condition provides us with the catalyst for taking action.

"Although we were physically located at the entrance of the Samarian city gate, we were very much part of the general condition prevailing at the time. We may not have made a pact with each other to eat our children as was the condition, but we felt the same hunger and despair as the people of Samaria.

"However, the important thing was that we realised this was not normal—this was a situation out of the ordinary caused primarily by the Syrians under the leadership of Ben Hadad. As God's chosen people, we were used to having everything we needed, including the very presence of God Himself.

"Thus, living a life of cannibalism was a far cry from the absolute protection and blessings we had enjoyed prior to this period. This is why we decided to do the unthinkable—go into the camp of our adversary and if *we perish, we perish.*

"As members of your communities, you have a mandate to do the unthinkable in order to get your generation out of the mess they often find themselves. The atmosphere and setting should give you no rest until you have taken those radical steps and made decisions, so like Esther, you can confidently say that if *I perish, I perish.*

Taking risks also involves knowing what the options are and still going for it.

"Having gone through the 'we must do something' stage, we were faced with the harsh reality of what was in store for us; what the real risks were and how we were going to handle them. When we assessed the risk, we said to each other:

"Why stay here and die? If we say, 'We'll go into the city,' the famine is there and we will die. And if we stay here, we will die. So let's go over to the camp of the Arameans and surrender. If they spare us, we live; if they kill us, then we die."
　2 Kings 7:4 (NIV)

"There was a degree of risk in all the options we had—with the potential of death either by starvation or at the hands of our enemy staring us in the face. Against the odds, we decided to swim against the current of popular opinion with all the consequences, and that decision made all the difference. In the end, we were able to fulfil our desire for comfort—all because we dared to be different!

"Your generation also faces some difficult choices ahead as they strive to settle into the life ordained for them. However, like us, they will have to take the road likely to be less travelled by, with all the detours, often going against the grain. This is what our Lord and Saviour would want us to do in following His example:

Your decision is the answer to a need.

"Many times, we do not recognise our decision to go against the grain, not only liberates others, thus setting them on the path to fulfilment, but also it is a general and passionate answer to a need.

"We did not know the decision we took would eventually usher in a period of abundance for the nation, and most importantly, fulfil a prophecy previously declared:

Elisha said, "Hear the word of the Lord. This is what the Lord says: about this time tomorrow, a seah of flour will sell for a shekel and two seahs of barley for a shekel at the gates of Samaria."
2 Kings 7:1 (NIV)

"With the benefit of hindsight, we were just making survival decisions. We never thought for a minute that we were the instruments God was using to bring about great redemption for the people of Samaria. It's amazing what God can do and the vessels He uses!

"If you have ever had doubts about the relevance and authenticity of risk-taking, remember that God uses our decisions as major instruments for the deliverance of an entire generation and situations. Do not settle for the comfortable things and comfortable places. Push yourself to the limit and beyond yourselves for, by doing so, you are setting the agenda for many other people; you are setting for them their *'about this time tomorrow ... moment.'*

God takes our obedience to instructions and transforms them into powerful weapons.

"We often do not know how powerful our risk-taking adventures are in the hands of the Author of life. We learnt this during our crucial decision-making time. We learnt it is often in those critical moments of taking action that He transforms our fears and anxieties into great weapons in His grand scheme of things.

"It was only when we 'got up and went to the camp of the Arameans' (2 Kings 7:5) that God brought about a miracle. For while we were tip-toeing towards the Aramean camp:

... the Lord had caused the Arameans to hear the sound of chariots and horses and a great army so that they said to one another, "Look, the king of Israel has hired the Hittite and Egyptian kings to attack us!"
So they got up and fled in the dusk and abandoned their tents and their horses and donkeys. They left the camp as it was and ran for their lives.
2 Kings 7:5–7 (NIV)

"It was when we started to act on our decision that the unexpected happened. God transformed the steps of four physically disabled men into 'the sound of chariots and horses and a great army.' All of this happened because we made a conscious decision to go against all human reason and opinion.

"In moments like these, the key is to act on the decisions you have made for God, whose works we cannot easily comprehend. He often uses what we are doing, however small or insignificant it might be, to bring about a great victory in the lives of people. Do not despise your risk-taking abilities; they are the lifeline to help establish the kingdom of God. Do not ignore it!"

We are lost for words at this moment as we take some time to ingest and digest what we have just heard. What makes it much more credible is that they come from a highly unlikely source. From the mouths of these men; men with huge physical challenges, have come timeless principles as well as words of wisdom which will stay with us forever.

What is fascinating is the fact that God used the footsteps of four leprous men to cause great fear and panic among the ranks of an entire army, and it testifies to who He is and what He does with broken and not-fit-for-purpose vessels.

One thing is sure after such a God-moment; we are more than ever ready to run our race. This time with a window for making life-changing decisions—ones that go against the current of popular opinion. As we ponder such an important message, they conclude by giving us parting words of wisdom:

Don't hesitate to take risk; you are the answer to a need.

"Just as our decision to step out of our comfort zone brought deliverance to Samaria, your decisions to take risks, both now and in the future, will bring vital answers to the many questions your generation faces. You are the answer to that problem of the young man and the young woman."

Don't be afraid to take risks. God will use them for a greater cause.

"You should feel confident in taking risks because God will turn those flawed, fearful decisions into the main source of redemption for your family and those closest to you. He will also use them to bring freedom and fulfilment to humanity. Don't ever forget this. He used our decision to bring an end to severe famine in which His people were reduced to cannibalism. And He is waiting for those who will dare to be different; for in your difference, you will find your sense of purpose.

Don't hesitate to take risks; it is for the common good.

"Our natural inclination is to feel we are solely responsible to ourselves for the decisions we take. This is not always the case. In fact, we must learn that the decisions we take, though on a personal level, have strong implications for the society we live in. Entire nations are freed or bound by the quality of the decisions you take. Having reached the 'promised land,' we soon realised the reason we were there—to liberate our people from starvation and thus usher in a period of abundance."

It is often when we take action that the breakthrough occurs.

"Making the decision to get out of our comfort zone is one thing, but acting out those tough decisions are the critical points in the process. And it is often when we act out those decisions that the floodgate of miracles opens. We are a living testimony."

Remember it is not always about you.

"Having come upon so much wealth and food, it was so easy for us to forget the reasons we were there. As we later pointed out to each other when we arrived at the Aramean camp, which was our 'promised land,' flowing with milk and honey:

"We're not doing right. This is a day of good news and we are keeping it to ourselves. If we wait until daylight, punishment will overtake us. Let's go at once and report this to the royal palace."
2 Kings 7:9 (NIV)

"We soon realised it was not about us; our fellow country men and women were also experiencing the same hunger and desperation. Rather than enjoying everything there was, we quickly came to our senses and shared the great news with the rest of the people. As a result, prophecy declared came to pass, and many people were saved."

With these words of wisdom, each one of them gives us a firm tap on the shoulders; a sign of encouragement as they make their way into the stands, among the other heroes who have encouraged and inspired us with their words of insight. We feel confident about the future—that with courage, discipline, and motivation, we will also be passing on these timeless principles to the next generation.

Before they leave, in unison, they offer up a prayer of encouragement for us:

Heavenly Father, thank you very much for the lives of these great men and women about to undertake the race of life.

Father, we pray that you will empower them with the courage to make decisions that will take them into the unknown where you are, so that through those decisions, you will be able to show them the unsearchable riches of your Kingdom which you have stored up for them.

Teach them to be confident of their decisions, knowing it is only when they are weak that they will be strong. This we ask in the name of your precious Son, Jesus, AMEN!

And with these parting words of prayer, they make their way out to be immediately followed by another great master.

In Summary

This is what the Four Lepers want you to know about living today from their life experience:

- Remember, taking risks is not always about you.

- An entire generation is waiting for you to take action. Their future liberation depends on it.
- Do not despise your current circumstances, for out of it will come forth a release of destinies.
- We are the answer to the prayers of people and nations. Do not underestimate your role in God's scheme of things.
- Your current circumstances provide the perfect opportunity for you to rise to your potential. Do not run away from it.

Chapter Eleven: The Hebrew Boys Stand Up for What You Believe

As the four lepers leave, we see three young men making their way towards us. We are left baffled as to who these young, smart-looking men are. Earlier on, we heard four leprous men encourage us to make in-roads into the unknown because that is where the promise of God is. We wonder what these young chaps have to say to us.

So far, we have heard from some great and yet ordinary men and women, just like you and me, who, through God, made history by highlighting the value of running with perseverance the race set before us while living in today's world. They all ran the race with determination, albeit they sometimes faltered along the way; yet they did not allow those temporary setbacks to stop them from reaching their goals.

These men and women never had the precedents to help them navigate the many challenges life threw at them, and yet, by cooperating with a greater source and power they were quick to recognise was God, were able to run successfully the journey marked out for them.

Some of them were able to defeat large superior armies with sophisticated weaponry with just a group of men who could best be described as "below amateurs." While in the process, however, they were able to unearth the incredible leadership potential inside of them. Others, were able to rally people behind them to rebuild broken walls which were more than just walls. They represented the power, autonomy, and sovereignty of a nation. And they did so under such intense pressure from an equally strong opposition who was happy with the status quo. All of these incredible achievements provide us with the needed morale booster as we put ourselves together to start all over again.

Looking back on all the people who have spoken, we can confidently say we stand a better chance of living our lives successfully today with their encouragement and wisdom. Why? Because, for once, we have all of these in the great cloud of witnesses who have gone before us and whose life journeys provide us with the blueprint.

Unlike us, Esther, Gideon, David, and Nehemiah did not have the benefit of all these role models and advice we have today. They had to work through trials and errors until they found how to start, maintain the momentum, and then finish the race successfully.

And, the best part of it is that these people were not super human beings. In fact, they have been described as men and women *with nature like ours* (James 5:17 NKJ), and yet they were able to do extraordinary things. These were men and women who were impulsive as some of us are, struggled with insecurities and low self-esteem as we do, and yet they were able to pray "earnestly" for drought and see results. Others were like Gideon, who, though insecure, was able to defeat the mighty Midianite army with 300 amateurs. If these individuals were able to do such incredible things, then we can do the same, if not better.

As they make their way towards us, we realise these men are from Babylon where the famous king Nebuchadnezzar once ruled a vast and wealthy kingdom. Are they going to tell us what this great king did during his reign? Are they going to tell us all the juicy gossip, of the magnificent architecture he built?

On closer inspection, we notice they are of Hebrew origin although they have Babylonian attire on. This can only be the Jewish boys who, through their resolute stance, stood up to Nebuchadnezzar, fully aware of the consequences. Is it Shadrach, Meshach and Abednego? Where is Daniel? He played a crucial role in their epic story.

As we keep guessing who they really are, one of them approaches us and says: *"You must stand up for what you believe in. You must not, under any circumstances, allow the world to dictate to you."* And before we get adjusted to what he is saying, he introduces himself as *Shadrach* ...

"Everyone knows me as Shadrach, but that is not my real name. My real name is Hananiah and, together with Daniel, Mishael, and Azariah, we were given different names as part of a rigorous assimilation policy of the Babylonian government aimed at making us lose our identity. This is what we want to tell you—people in the world work to cause you to lose your identity and to keep you from being who God created you to be. The world's system works frantically to get you to forget the truth about who you are and in whose image you have been created, but we are here to encourage you to stand up for what you believe in.

"The world often sets the agenda for our lives. Unfortunately, most of what it is selling as the ideal life is not what they make it to be. Quite to the contrary, it is the counterfeit ideal often disguised as the status quo. Many people have tried to live this lie but it hasn't got them anywhere.

There is such a thing as *the* original ideal life. It is one based on having God as the foundation and living each day according to His instructions. This is what we ought to strive for. And when we do catch on to it, we have a duty to defend it by standing up for it, even if it means being martyred as a result of defending the truth. We speak from experience."

These are strong words to take in. He continues...

"We were Hebrews taken into captivity in Babylon as a result of our disobedience to God. And, as if being in exile as a refugee was not enough, King Nebuchadnezzar had other ideas in mind for us.

"He initiated a huge recruitment drive aimed at getting the best minds into his civil service. In particular, he looked to find among the exiles, young, energetic, and intelligent men and women who would help keep the wheels of his government running. This is the account of the way the recruitment drive was done:

Then the king ordered Ashpenaz, chief of his court officials, to bring in some of the Israelites from the royal family and the nobility—young men without any physical defects, handsome, showing aptitude for every kind of learning, well informed, quick to understand and qualified to serve in the king's palace.

He was to teach them the language and literature of the Babylonians
Daniel 1:3-4 (NIV)

"King Nebuchadnezzar had a taste for the best of everything, and this was evident in the calibre of people he looked for to serve in his administration. But why the desire for young, Hebrew people? This is a question I have wondered for quite some time.

"While I may not know the reasons why he specifically wanted us, we can safely say that it was one elaborate programme which went beyond recruitment to the civil service. It also served as a detailed programme of integration in which we were meant to become Babylonians in everything except the way we looked. This is what one would describe as a total assimilation."

Abednego continued...

"Shadrach is spot on in describing what went on back then. It is reminiscent of what is happening in your generation.

"A careful observation of social trends points towards a subtle, but aggressive acculturation going on, symbolised by the worldly ideology in which many people, including, *'people of the household of faith,'* have been sapped into it. The mention of a one-world government with its economic system championed by world leaders is no coincidence. This happened during the Babylonian empire.

"The world system aggressively embarked on a recruitment exercise aimed at making young men and women *'without physical defect, handsome and showing aptitude for every kind of learning, well-informed, quick to understand and qualified to serve in the king's palace'* assimilated into the system being built.

"They also sought people who would speak one language—the language of the world, which often plagiarises God's original ideal of life, the relativity of truth, questions about the existence of God and such other lies and deceit, as it deems fit.

"This is the point of diversion we want to bring to your attention." Abednego continues...

"Although we went through the recruitment process, we still maintained our integrity. In fact, we did not allow our knowledge of the truth to be destroyed. We stood firm for what we believed in.

"Contrary to what the world would have us believe, there is an absolute truth out there—one which helped us overcome the many obstacles we faced as a result of standing firm for what we believed in. Our brother and friend, Daniel, who was one of us, also went through some difficulties with us as well as on his own.

"To illustrate the pressure we faced, the following are a few examples to help encourage you, as well as strengthen your resolve to hold on to the truth no matter what the circumstances may be."

The Spirit of Compromise

"A keen observer of your world can easily conclude that, if there was ever a contagious bug spreading around today, it is the bug of compromise. And such is the level of compromise that the line between truth and falsehood is blurred, or, in some cases, non-existent. We were faced with the same situation.

"When Nebuchadnezzar embarked on his recruitment drive, aimed particularly among the Hebrew population, the intention was for us to lose our identity as the chosen people of God. We had the ability to know the truth about who we were as a people and also the natural laws established by God as the basis for living.

"In today's terms, that would amount to total acculturation, thus making us '*Babylonians in Hebrew skins.*'

"We would have compromised our identity, culture, language, and other aspects which made us unique. This is precisely when we decided to do something about it. We were determined to hold on to the truth as we knew it would eventually set us free. There was every indication that they were going to be successful in what they had set out to achieve:

- They changed our Hebrew names for Babylonian ones—Daniel became Belteshazzar, Hananiah

became Shadrach, Meshael to Meshach, and I, Azariah, became Abednego.
- We went through three years of training in Babylonian literature and the arts. This was to ensure we were fully integrated into the Babylonian society.

"We had compromise written over everything we did and everywhere we went. But we did not allow that to sway us.

"Unlike what they expected, we held on firmly to the truth and the other beliefs we had been brought up with. Like Daniel, we *'resolved not to defile ourselves with the royal food and wine ...'* (Daniel 1:8). Looking back on it, it was not an easy decision to take, but we knew we had to do it.

"Inspired by Daniel, we all opted for simple vegetables and water during the training period rather than the daily portion of food given out by Nebuchadnezzar, much of which was offered to pagan gods. The result was evident for all to see, including Ashpenaz, who had put his job, reputation, and life on the line for us. It is recorded in the scripture that:

And at the end of the ten days, they looked healthier and better nourished than any of the young men who ate the royal food.
   Daniel 1:15 (NIV)

"We had to take a stand in not allowing ourselves to be contaminated by the dysfunction of what Nebuchadnezzar offered. And herein lies the secret.

"Because of our resolve, God gave us favour in the eyes of Ashpenaz, who was able to go along with our plan. Again, the evidence was there for all to see after the training programme was over. Our God gave us *'knowledge and skill in all literature and wisdom,'* and Daniel, in particular, had the gift of understanding in all visions and dreams.

"When you decide to take a stand for what you believe in, especially when such convictions are in line with God's overall will and purpose for your life, all heaven comes in to help you win your case against the powers that be. In our case, it brought us favour and promotion in a foreign land. What an incredible story!

"And to make things conclusive, when we were interviewed by the king himself to determine our suitability for the job on hand, he found there were none like us. Besides, when it came to matters of wisdom and understanding about which the king examined us, he found us ten times better than all the magicians and astrologers in his kingdom. This is what happens when we stand up for what we believe in.

"Your generation is looking for people who, like Daniel, will not defile themselves with what is happening around them, most of which is not in line with their purpose and aspirations or God's overall purpose for them. Like us, you need a strong conviction to say *NO* to what the world tells you.

"Remember, when you stand for what you believe in, there is always a divine favour that comes upon you, which enables you to do things you never thought of doing."

At this stage, a strong sense of conviction and faith begins to build in us. We begin asking ourselves, "What do I stand for? Is it in line with my dreams and aspirations? Most importantly, is it in line with God's overall purpose for my life?" Our communities need the Shadrachs, Meshachs and Abednegos of this world!

Just as we begin to re-examine our core values, Meshach steps out and continues...

"What Abednego has just described to you is one hurdle we had to overcome, but it was by no means the only one. The next challenge was the biggest one we ever faced; a challenge which ultimately brought us greater favour and a greater promotion. Thus, we discovered that the level of our challenge determined the level of promotion. The same goes for you."

This is incredible wisdom coming from such a reliable and credible source of strength and encouragement.

"When we excelled in our first challenge, we were promoted to serve at the heart of the Babylonian government structure. The deeper the challenge, the higher the level of promotion we received and the greater the glory, which went to God because He had given us the favour, gifts, and talents to enable us to serve in a worldly system such as the one in Babylon.

"However, our biggest challenge, one which was to ultimately define who we were, was about to unfold. Our lives were never going to be the same."

The Golden Image

"King Nebuchadnezzar made a golden image, the height of which was 'sixty cubits and its width were six cubits' (Daniel 3:1). He wanted the entire Babylonian population to acknowledge it as the new national deity. Subsequently, at the dedication service, everyone was required to bow down and worship the image. If someone failed to do so, he or she would be condemned to death by burning in a furnace.

"This was clearly another attempt to make us worship a creature rather than the Creator. This was a clear violation of the fifth commandment God gave us back on Mount Sinai under Moses's leadership:

You shall not make for yourself a carved image – any likeness of anything that is in heaven above or that is in the water under the earth;

You shall not bow down to them nor serve them. For I, the Lord your God, am a jealous God visiting the iniquity of the fathers upon the children to the third and fourth generation of those who hate me.
Deuteronomy 5:8-9 (NKJV)

"For us, this was a straightforward situation we found ourselves in. Because the command from the king was in breach of our fundamental core values, it was quite easy for us to defy the royal edict with its consequences. The consequences of our action, or, better still, inactions, were not easy to deal with. However, help was on hand when we needed it.

"Our disobedience was reported to the king, who wanted to hear and see it first-hand, so we were summoned before him. Right before the king, we stood up for our core values and thus defied his instruction. This is what we said:

Shadrach, Meshach and Abednego replied to the king, "O Nebuchadnezzar, we do not need to defend ourselves before you in this matter. If we are thrown into the blazing furnace, the God we serve is able to save us from it, and he will rescue us from your hands, O king."
Daniel 3:16-17 (NIV)

"I know you might be thinking this was a really brave and confident effort coming from us. We had the guts to defy the most powerful king at the time. And the answer is yes, we did!

"For us, we were prepared to do what it took to stand up for what we believed in. You should also be able to do the same—in fact, we dare you to take a stand for what you believe in!

"Where did our confidence come from? Our confidence came from above. Following the success of our initial challenge with the food, we were confident God was with us all the time, and we knew He was ready to come to our rescue whenever we made decisions and took steps that would bring glory to His name.

"Any time you make a choice that glorifies His name at the expense of the world's system, He is always there to bring you into favour with the powers that be. This is part of His nature—to fight and defend the things that bring glory to His name.

"And with this confidence we were prepared to put our lives on the line, even if God did not save us. This confidence led us to make this emphatic statement:

"But even if he does not, we want you to know, O king, that we will not serve your gods or worship the image of gold you have set up."
Daniel 3:18 (NIV)

"Even if, for argument's sake, God was not going to save us, we were still going ahead with a stance of obedience to God. This made the next action look rather like child's play. The punishment for our action was for us to be bound and put into a fiery furnace heated seven times the normal temperature.

"Although we were bound and put in a fiery furnace, we were not burnt and neither were any hairs on our heads singed. We had the company of a fourth man who Nebuchadnezzar described as *'the son of God'* (Daniel 3:25) with us. This is what the power of conviction can do when you harness its potential."

With those words, we are left in awe of these guys who, as we have just heard, went through quite a traumatic experience, but who were also excited to share with us.

As we ponder on their experiences, we wonder whether we can also be bold and confident enough to go against the grain. How many people in our communities have taken such a stance in their lives?

For many of us the idea of moving out of our comfort zones scares us to death. But we've got these Hebrew guys on hand to encourage us. Our generation, communities, and nations need people like Shadrach, Meshach, and Abednego to change our societies for the better.

As we are left to digest the words of these incredible men, they offer us their parting wisdom.

"Always remember that:

God honours those who put their life on the line for His glory.

"There is something about a soul that honours God. Because we stood up for our core values based on God's principles and divine wisdom, He was on hand to defend us even to the point of death.

"So don't be afraid to lay your life on the line to defend what you believe to be Godly wisdom. Quite frankly, the world needs people like you.

The greater the level of challenge, the higher the level of promotion.

"When you do not give in to the challenges that come from standing up for what you believe in, there is often a promotion at the door. And the greater the challenges you face, the higher the level of promotion you will receive.

"When we made the decision not to eat the daily ration the king provided, but instead just to eat vegetables and water, we were healthier and wiser than those who had taken in double and triple portions of the ration. As a result, we were fast-tracked into the Babylonian civil service.

Continue to stand for what you believe in even if it doesn't make sense.

"We were so confident that we were willing to put our lives on the line, even if God was not going to save us. It did not make sense, but we were still ready to go for it. Such should be your resolve that you will do anything it takes, even if it does not make sense to people."

And with those last words, they make their way out. But before they leave, they introduce the next person.

"We are sure you will be encouraged by the next person. He was part of us and also experienced the same things we faced. Daniel will share with you some of life's important lessons—and, in particular, how to develop a spirit of excellence." With those words, they leave to be followed by Daniel.

In Summary

This is what the Hebrew boys want you to know about living today from their life experiences:

- When you stand up for what you believe in, the world takes notice of you. In our case, a decree acknowledging our God as the most powerful deity on earth was passed throughout the whole of Babylon.
- Remember that the deeper the level of challenge, the higher the level of promotion. When you hold on to what you believe in, there is usually promotion at the door for you.
- When you stand for values that are in line with Godly principles and wisdom, God comes to

your aid in granting you favour in the eyes of the powers that be.
- Even if there is no backing to what you believe in, still stand.

Chapter Twelve: Daniel
Developing a Spirit of Excellence

Daniel, perhaps more than any other person, deserves to bring encouragement and Godly wisdom to us. He, like most of the heroes who have spoken to us so far, has walked through and experienced more difficult situations than the average person has in a lifetime and yet was still able to overcome them all. He faced many life-changing moments, moments that would have ended many a life.

We would probably never have heard of his story, let alone read about him in scripture, if he hadn't endured and overcome those challenges. And yet, through the protection and strength from God, he was able to make life-changing decisions that changed an entire political, social, and religious landscape.

With Daniel, we can confidently say we are in for a good time together, a time of encouragement and enrichment. As if what we've heard so far is not enough, we are about to be taken to a whole new level of bravery; something definitely not for the faint-hearted, but needed among the emerging generation of today.

We've heard first-hand accounts of what went on in Babylon under King Nebuchadnezzar and some of the difficult, but vital life decisions, the Hebrew boys had to make. As we meditate and take in what they have told us, we wonder whether Daniel will repeat what Shadrach, Meshach, and Abednego have already told us. Will Daniel give us a different and unique insight into what really happened in captivity and how they coped with it?

Or perhaps, he will give his perspective on the numerous brushes he had with the Babylonian system and the various punishments he received. In particular, is he going to tell us how it felt to be in the midst of ferocious animals like lions in a den?

We are truly excited because, whatever he decides to tell us, there will be a powerful, life-transforming message that will come out of it; something to further encourage and equip us as we gather momentum to live today.

As we ponder over all we have heard, Daniel approaches with a firm tap on our shoulders and begins to encourage us ...

"Your world is in dire need of men and women who are not afraid to stand up for what they believe in. But in order to really impart knowledge and make an impact on your city, neighbourhood, and community, you need to develop a spirit of excellence. This is what will enable you to get audiences with the message of God's purpose for people.

"I know my brothers and fellow countrymen have told you of all the challenges we faced and how we managed to go through those hurdles, thereby moving us from the pits to the pinnacles of the Babylonian system. But I am here to encourage you that an excellent spirit can give you the necessary voice and authority to turn your society around in line with God's will. The good news is you don't have to be an extraordinary person to have an excellent spirit.

"You have heard from Gideon about the hero in you waiting to manifest. Like him, developing an excellent spirit will get you divine favours which will enable you to perform to your capacity.

"As refugees living in captivity in Babylon, there were many policies, strategies and programmes aimed at making us lose our sense of identity, and most importantly, our relationship with God as my brothers mentioned earlier. But again, having a spirit of excellence made us stand apart from the rest and also gave us favour with the powers that be. To illustrate how this was carried out, here are a few examples of how having an excellent spirit set us apart."

Developing the spirit of excellence gave us fast access into the king's service.

"When we were drafted into the recruitment programme, by which qualified applicants would enter the king's service, we were allocated daily food rations as part of the process. However, we remained true to our ancestral roots by courteously refusing *'the royal food and wine'* (Daniel 1: 8) because it was tainted with idolatry. Also, the rations were contrary to the Levitical purity laws.

"Furthermore, our integrity simply forbade us to a life of compromise in which we were going to throw away what was the very source of our life in exchange for something worldly. After having vegetables and water, we were found ten times healthier and wiser than our peers, who had double portions of the king's ration. This led to us being fast-tracked into the king's service."

Developing a spirit of excellence enabled us to step into our gifts, talents, and skills.

"Because we were in sync with God's spirit, which had become part of our daily life, we were able to identify our core gifts, talents, and skills that had already been deposited in us. Not only were we able to identify them, but we were also able to use them to establish the purposes of God in Babylon at the time. Scripture explicitly records that:

To these four young men God gave knowledge and understanding of all kinds of literature and learning. And Daniel could understand visions and dreams of all kinds.

In every matter of wisdom and understanding about which the king questioned them, he found them ten times better than all the magicians and enchanters in his whole kingdom.
Daniel 1:17-20 (NIV)

"Being in touch with our core skills and talents enabled us to deploy them which, in turn, brought us favour, so we could set God's agenda in a very 'Babylonian' system. We were very much aware of our mandate, so we were prepared to step into it."

Having an excellent spirit brought on challenges which led to our promotion.

"This is the fun part of everything we endured during our time in Babylon. Having an excellent spirit, among other things, included not compromising our fundamental core values, even if it meant putting our lives on the line. We were given the opportunity to demonstrate our non-compromising stance.

"King Nebuchadnezzar built a golden image which was to be honoured as the official deity of the kingdom—a clear violation of the fifth commandment, which prevented us from making any graven image or bowing down or worshiping it. We would rather worship the Creator than a creature, clearly made by human hands.

"When we defied the king's orders to bow down and worship the golden image, we were put in a burning furnace heated seven times the normal temperature. But again, help was at hand.

"Because of our excellent spirit in not compromising our core values, God was on hand to save us from being burnt. And the result of this ordeal? It prompted the king to pass a law making the God of Israel, the Creator of the universe, as the official state deity in Babylon. This is how the scripture recorded it:

Then Nebuchadnezzar said, "Praise be to the God of Shadrach, Meshach and Abednego who has sent his angels and rescued his servants. They trusted in Him and defied the king's command and were willing to give up their lives rather than serve or worship any god except their own God.

Therefore, I decree that the people of my nation or language who say anything against the God of Shadrach, Meshach and Abednego be cut into pieces and their houses be turned into piles of rubble for no other god can save in this way."

Daniel 3:28-29 (NIV)

"Thus, our decision not to bow down to the golden image was a test to find out which deity was the best. In the end, we were vindicated because our God came to our rescue prompting the king to acknowledge that there was no better God in all the earth except the God of Abraham, Isaac, and Jacob, who also happened to be the God whom my fellow countrymen and I served.

"Your world is in need of people who, by not defiling themselves with worldly dysfunction, can develop the excellent spirit needed to bring order, righteousness, and integrity into the culture."

"The world is in need of men and women who, among other things, will:

Through an excellent spirit identify their fundamental core values and be prepared to defend them with their lives. We did it and succeeded in showing the world that what we believed in was wholesome enough to turn whole societies and nations around for the best.

Through an excellent spirit identify and develop core gifts, talents, skills, and abilities they have been endowed with. Sadly, there are many people who are not in tune with the potential within them. Each and every one of us has been given gifts and talents (Ephesians 4:7-8) for the purpose of preparing as well as equipping people so that, together, we can all live effective and productive lives. I was given the gift of interpreting dreams and the gift of prophecy.

"Remember Joseph earlier on, when he came into his calling by interpreting the dreams of Pharaoh. Not only did he succeed in shedding light on a very difficult-to-understand dream, but also his gift took him into prominence and before kings. When I interpreted Nebuchadnezzar's dreams, it stopped the wholesale execution of the top advisors in Babylon (Daniel 2: 24-49) and also brought God into the national agenda, even if it was a brief period.

"This was a significant event which again brought God into the national consciousness in Babylon and helped shape the way we related to Him in a very special way.

"So, as you can see, it is very important to identify your core values and gifts, for this will bring you into prominence, and most importantly, bring glory to the originator of those gifts."

The Lion's Den

"Several years ago, Solomon, undoubtedly the wisest king ever to have ruled Israel, made an observation about the value of having an excellent spirit. He also made an interesting observation about what our skills, gifts, and talents could do for us. He said:

Do you see a man skilled in his work? He will serve before kings; he will not serve before obscure men.
Proverbs 22:29 (NIV)

"He was and still is absolutely right when he made this observation. I was a living testimony to what he had written years before I had come on the scene, and yet I experienced it!

"I then came to the conclusion that everything you see on the pages of what is undoubtedly the greatest book ever written on Earth—the Bible—is true. I encourage you not to take the truths and wisdom in the book for granted because they are *THE TRUTH!*

"Because of my excellent spirit, which saw me step into my core gifts, talents, and skills, I was elevated to one of the highest positions in Babylon. The scripture records that:

It pleased Darius to appoint 120 satraps to rule throughout the kingdom with three administrators over them, one of whom was Daniel. The satraps were made accountable to them so that the king might not suffer loss.
Daniel 6: 1-2 (NIV)

"Such is the level of trust King Darius had that he was prepared to entrust the main responsibilities of efficiently running the kingdom to me and the two other administrators.

"The question I have been asked, and which you might be inclined to ask, is why would Darius entrust me and the others with such important responsibilities? After all, I'm only a foreigner or, worse still, a refugee living in Babylon.

"He felt it safe to entrust us with running the kingdom. Besides, having distinguished myself over the period, he was confident I could lead and run the country effectively without him suffering any loss.

"Just like Joseph and others before me, those years of serving the good and not-so-good leaders were a period of testing and character building. I was able to serve succeeding kings over a period with integrity and hard work. This, in turn, fire-proofed me, leading other kings to believe I was qualified enough to be entrusted with the responsibility of efficiently running the kingdom's affairs.

"One can also safely say that my track record was there for all to see, as scriptures rightly point out:

Now Daniel so distinguished himself among the administrators and the satraps because an excellent spirit was in him and the king gave thought to setting him over the whole realm.
Daniel 6:3 (NKJV)

"My gifts and skills set me up to stand before kings and not mere men. However, this opportunity was not going to happen without a fight! As I later learnt, sometimes the fight strikes at the core of what you believe in, especially when there is no other way to get to you. There were a few of the satraps and administrators who, not happy at the thought of having a Hebrew refugee running the kingdom, wanted to bring me down.

"Now, because I had distinguished myself over the years with the roles and responsibilities I had been entrusted with, they could not find any 'dirt' on me. The scripture records that:

At this, the administrators and the satraps tried to find grounds for charges against Daniel in his conduct of government affairs but they were unable to do so. They could find no

corruption in him because he was trustworthy and neither corrupt nor negligent.
Daniel 6: 4 (NIV)

"Now, herein lies the secret; you will only be able to move from one level of greatness to another when you have excelled at the level you're at. Can you imagine what would have happened if they had found anything wrong with my work? My integrity would have been called to question and, most importantly, I would have brought shame and disgrace to the one who had blessed me with those gifts and skills.

"These conspirators who wanted to bring me down would have succeeded in their agenda if I had allowed sloppiness and mediocrity to define who I was and what I was about.

"A life of compromise and mediocrity is very easy to live. For people who live in this parallel universe, moving out of their comfort zones into a realm of excellence involves a higher price they would rather not pay. This is the whole essence of having all those in the *cloud of witnesses* to encourage and push you to get out of your comfort zone. Remember, God works with those who are willing and prepared to push the boundaries of their comfort zones.

"Because they could not find fault in my professional duties, they struck at the core of my fundamental values and beliefs. In other words, since they were not going to find anything pertaining to my level of commitment to the cause or my style of administration, they were going to hit me where it hurt the most—my relationship with God:

Finally these men said, "We will never find any basis for charges against this man Daniel unless it has something to do with the law of his God."

Daniel 6:5 (NIV)

"And they succeeded by having the king to enact a law making it illegal for anyone to pray to and worship anyone, divine or human, except the king, a decree I was definitely going to disobey. Knowing this, they came to my home and found me defying the order. As a result, I was put in a den with ferocious lions. But again, God showed up!

"Because I had taken a stand for Him, He came to my rescue by shutting the mouth of the hungry lions. When I was lifted out of the den, '*no wound was found on him because he had trusted in his God*' **(Daniel 6: 23)."**

There is a standing ovation as a sign of respect to someone who has been through a barrage of challenges. How many of us can confidently say we have gone through such challenges? Yet, in speaking into our lives, he has succeeded in sowing seeds of faith and encouragement into us. For someone to be put in a den full of hungry lions and yet remain safe is a great testament to what a person with such strong conviction can do.

Daniel's story of courage and divine wisdom is one we all need for this hour. Our generation needs to hear such stories of sheer conviction, courage, and perseverance.

As Daniel makes his way out, he leaves us with these incredible words of wisdom:

Living an excellent life makes you live beyond reproach.

"Identifying and developing an excellent spirit places you in a unique position in which you live beyond reproach. Many dreams and destinies have been brought to an abrupt end because lives were not lived with a spirit of excellence.

"As a result, people and other conspirators have a field day striking at the core of who we are. They tried this on me, but because I had these unique qualities that set me apart, I was able to live above their plans and strategies to bring me down. There are conspirators who are waiting to point fingers and find faults with what you do. Don't give them the chance!"

Identifying and developing your core skills, gifts, and talents will bring you into prominence.

"The person who knows what they have and steps into it is likely to stand in prominence. I am a living example. Similarly, people who do not know what they've got will walk around aimlessly without living a life of significance. In some cases, they live a life of poverty."

Developing an excellent spirit will bring you into conflict with people.

"But when this happens, there is no need to be afraid as help is at hand. Because you have taken a stand for what you believe in, God will come to your rescue, and you can be rest assured that he will come through for you."

With these words, Daniel makes way for the next hero. We are reaching our peak with such incredible words of wisdom and courage from these great men and women who have seen and done it all. There is no way we can fail after hearing such a great cloud of witnesses.

In Summary

This is what the Daniel wants you to know about living today from his life experience:

- Developing an excellent spirit will open doors and bring you into prominence. Know, however, that this is not for your ego. It is for God's glory to be manifested through you. He gets all the credit!

- Developing an excellent spirit will enable you to step into your core gifts, talents, skills, and abilities. This is what will bring you into prominence.
- Through an excellent spirit, you identify your core values. Identifying them will also give you the courage to defend them whatever the situation.
- And you are always assured of God's presence to defend you when you come under attack for your values. He always delights in people who stand up for what they believe in.
- Having an excellent spirit will also bring you into conflict with those who do not share the same ideals. The only solution is to keep doing what you are doing and leave the problem to God.

Chapter Thirteen:
The Persistent Widow
Persistence Pays

The woman approaching us looks like someone who's gone through many agonising and frustrating moments in her life. There is, however, an air of justice, vindication and satisfaction about her, almost as if she's been fighting the war of life for a long time, but has finally won the battle, giving her a sense of accomplishment. As she makes her way to address us, we wonder what she will tell us.

Who is she? She seems like a relatively unknown person. This is because all the giants of the faith who have addressed us have been known for what they did during their time on Earth—Daniel, Esther, and Joseph, just to mention a few. But we do not know this relatively unknown woman and what she has for us.

Just as we get into a reflective moment, she addresses us.

"I may be an old woman, relatively unknown to many of you, but I'm excited about what I want to share with you; something I have no doubt will equip you for the rest of your race in your life journey."

Our faces light up with shock and surprise, but also excitement. We can't wait to hear what she has to say to us

"Earlier you were encouraged by the story of Jabez, who was able to rewrite the next chapters of his life, which turned out to be far better than the darkness that surrounded his birth and early life. I know he mentioned prayer and confession of faith as the weapons he discovered in his life-transforming experience.

"My encouragement is that, when you pray and confess all the good things God has planned and purposed in your life, it sometimes takes time from the prayer and confession to its manifestation. When that happens, all you have to do is to develop persevering muscles.

"Persistence really pays off! If you will persist in knocking on the doors of heaven through your prayers and confessions of the truth, the door will definitely open for you. At least, this is what I learnt when I went through a similar situation.

"I know you are wondering who I really am since I am not mentioned much in the Bible; neither am I one of the major characters in the scriptures, but my life experience was so compelling that Jesus Christ used my story to illustrate to His disciples and also to those gathered around about a lesson in persistence, as is recorded in Luke 18:1-8.

"Jesus, through my experience (in a parable), reiterated the importance of praying and persevering, even when there is no sign of your request being granted. He compared Himself as the saviour and supplier of all our needs to an unrighteous judge who, in spite of his disregard for God and man, was forced to grant my wishes after I had persistently wore Him down.

"In the parable, there was a judge who *'neither feared God nor cared about men'* (Luke 18: 1). I had a problem with an adversary which needed settlement, albeit in my favour. But here lies the moral of the story.

"Although I had pressed for justice for my cause, the judge did not pay any attention to me. Each day, I was the first person at his chambers and the last person to leave. But he was not swayed by my enthusiasm to see justice done in my case.

"I had to persist and persevere to the very end. I left no stone unturned in my quest to see justice done. With the benefit of hindsight, I'm quite sure his paralegal became sick and tired of me with the occasional 'here she comes again' looks. I'm quite sure I had become a rather unpopular person and the subject of much gossip at the court, but that did not stop me from getting what I wanted.

"Such is the level of my persistence that I literally wore the judge out, prompting him to make this statement:

... even though I don't fear God or care about men, yet because this widow keeps bothering me, I will see that she gets justice so that she won't eventually wear me out with her coming."
Luke 18:4-5 (NIV)

"The key to my success in getting what was rightfully mine was the persistence in getting justice done. Jesus similarly reiterated that, if an unjust judge is able to grant the wishes and desires for me, how much more will a loving father give you your heart's desires?

"Jesus, by using my example, was teaching people one of life's vital lessons—do not give up on seeing the fulfilment of God's will until it's been answered, for it will surely be granted. This lesson goes way beyond prayers and getting justice done for a poor old widow!

"The life application of this parable is that, when we desire something, for as long as our desires are in line with God's overall will and purpose, He is ready to grant them to us. Remember, He did it for Jabez, and He will do it for you. He's already done it for many people, and you are certainly not going to be the last person.

"As you go about living your life, always remember that you have weapons which will help you lay aside all the 'weights' and the sins which easily entangle, so that you can run with perseverance the race marked out for you. Don't ever forget this!"

What an awesome word coming from an amazing woman! Her story provides us with such a powerful lesson we will definitely need. We are going to hit some rocks on our way, but as we have just heard, if we continue 'drilling' through those obstacles, we will soon be on the other side.

Before she leaves, she prays for us:

Jesus, thank you for the lives of these precious souls as they endeavour to run their race of life. Lord, I pray they will be reminded of your desire to see them prosper and be all that you created them to be. And when they feel like giving up at any point, encourage them with my story and the need to persevere. For, as you demonstrated, persistence pays.

Thank you, Lord, for what you have accomplished in them, AMEN.

And with those words, she gives us a kiss of encouragement and makes her way from us. In the distance, we see another giant of the faith coming to address us.

In Summary

This is what the Persistent Widow wants you to know about living today from her life experience:
- Never give up on your dreams. Keep knocking, and the door will be opened unto you.
- Do not allow the circumstances of life to convince you to abandon your dreams. They are

there to strengthen and not to make us lose heart.
- Remember that God is not like the unjust judge. He gives gifts to those He loves, which includes you!

Chapter 14:
Paul
Discover Your Purpose

We almost feel ready to face the world. After listening to such incredible stories of sheer determination, courage, and wisdom, we are strengthened to not let anything stand in our way. We are ready to live Godly, productive lives. This, we'll do by running with perseverance the race set before us and leave a legacy for future generations in the process.

There is everything to pursue: holiness, righteousness, success, and strong relationships both with our Creator and with fellow man, as well as achieving one's dreams, goals, and aspirations.

Listening to such great words of wisdom and support from outstanding men and women who have transformed the political, social, economic, and religious landscape of the Earth over several centuries, we know we are in good company. Even if we falter along the way, which we will do from time to time, we have these in the great cloud of witnesses to help us stay on our feet.

There were times when these men and women, just like us, thought they were failures. Gideon thought so—that there was no way he could master the leadership qualities needed to put an army together to fight the mighty Midianites. He struggled with all the insecurities. And yet, in the mist of all the negativity, he was enabled with power and confidence from God to do the unexpected. With only three hundred less-than-convincing men, he was able to defeat giants.

Through Gideon, we are once again reminded that we are all mighty heroes and heroines awaiting our manifestation. Inside each one of us is an incredible power and ability to create a new world for ourselves and for generations to come. If only we could shake off our old mentality and the stereotypes we are often labelled with, our world would be a better place.

With such energy and excitement bursting out of us, we can't wait to go out there and rewrite our destinies, as well as the destinies of others. For now more than ever before, we know that changing our destinies will invariably have an effect on the lives of others.

For the "Sarahs" of this world, they are constantly reminded by Jabez that one can rewrite their life's script regardless of the circumstances in which they find themselves. They don't have to accept what the popular culture represented by society tells them.

However, despite what we've already heard, there is one more nugget of wisdom to receive before we take on the world. And perhaps, more than anyone else, this giant of the faith has the moral duty to seal everything we have heard so far with his parting wisdom.

Who is this giant of the faith? What has he got that the heroes before him haven't given us? We have received powerful testimonies and insights of how lives were transformed under incredible odds. So what next? Is there anything new under the sun?

There is a sudden burst of applause all around us, which becomes a standing ovation. For a minute, it seem as though we are witnessing the end of an incredible theatrical performance when the cast appears for the final curtain call. But no! It is not a theatrical performance as we would believe, nor is it to applaud a Thespian.

Rather, the applause is for a man who, judging from the reception, is someone who has incredible integrity and commands respect. He walks with such authority and with an enormous sense of respect as someone who has experienced a lot of hardship and opposition. But just like the ones before him, there is a sense of vindication and fulfilment written on his face. This can only be someone who is significant to our race of life and has been on the journey we're embarking on; full of uncertainties and questions.

While we are left to ponder and try to figure out who he really is, he speaks to us...

"I am Paul. Many of you know me as the Apostle, and I want to share with you of my experience and lessons learnt for your journey ahead."

All of a sudden, there is silence as we come to terms with what we are about to hear. This is the man credited for authoring almost half of the New Testament, part of unarguably the greatest, authority and most widely read book on Earth. Such a gifted communicator and a fluid writer, we feel honoured to hear him speak to us.

No one in history apart from Jesus Christ has the moral authority to speak to us as Paul does. His letters or Epistles have brought power and inspiration to millions of people over the centuries and certainly to us. Indeed, from his Epistles, many lives have been transformed positively for the cause of Christ; not to speak of the volumes of healing and freedom it has brought to people. Because of Paul's writings, many people have come to embrace the saving grace of Jesus Christ; all that He did for mankind and its implications for us today.

But what is he going to tell us? There is so much he could share. Is he going to shed light on his experience on the road to Damascus where he travelled with intent to carry out his plan of mass persecution of the early church? Or perhaps, he will share the secret and joys of making the truth of the gospel known to mankind; how he went about it, often facing hostile opposition to his beliefs.

We still do not know what's in store for us with Paul, although we are certain that we will not be the same after such an encounter. I feel confident we are about to be released into our purpose and fulfilment.

Paul begins ..."Each one of you is born for a life of purpose. For some of you, this becomes apparent during the early stages of your life, while for others, it takes a long time to grab hold of this. Most often, it is when you have gone through a path you thought was the best, but you were not experiencing the fulfilment you were born to have; that is when you began your search. I am here to assure you it is fine to step out and take a leap of faith.

"In fact, for some of you, this will not make sense at this moment, and this, too, is perfectly fine. But learn from me today that in spite of all these beliefs and thoughts, you have been ordained with a purpose; one you will fulfil before you finally depart from this world. So that like me, when you have accomplished your purpose, you can confidently conclude that you have fought the fight, finished the race, and stand ready for the crown which awaits you in heaven!"

We can sense the momentum building as Paul sets the stage for what is to come.

"I am living proof of a life that was lived with a sense of purpose and focus. I have been credited with penning almost half of the New Testament. While this is true, I can say with absolute certainty that I was only able to achieve this because as I once pointed out to King Agrippa, I was not disobedient to the vision from heaven. Indeed, I was only able to do what I did because I cooperated with God on what He wanted to accomplish on Earth—filling the Earth with the good news of his grace and salvation.

"However, this was not always the case. At a point in my life, I was disobedient to the heavenly vision for my life. To put it bluntly, I did not know what my life's purpose was until a chain of events opened my eyes to this all-important subject of vision. Or at least, what I thought was my life's purpose was not at all what it was.

Persecution without Measure

"I used to be part of the 'establishment' that opposed the theology and doctrines of the followers of Christ. My education in Judaism placed me in a unique position where I saw the big chasm—one that existed between the official state religion at the time and a new wave of teaching. This wave was espoused by Jesus Christ and adhered to by his followers who became known as Christians.

"Such was the level of persecution we meted out to the Christians that there was no way out for them. Saul, as I was called back then, got letters of approval from the Bishops and High Priests of the establishment so I could go on a state-sponsored mission of persecuting and in some cases, arresting Christians and having them imprisoned.

"Looking back on it, I see how I relished my new-found zeal and exploited my authority. The mention of my name struck fear in the heart of many Christians. I am sure they must have wondered why such a vicious man would want to hunt them down like game. But that was exactly how it looked."

My Damascus Moment

"I now realize all of this was for nothing. It was as if I had been running for many miles but to nowhere. I thought I was doing everything by the book, and for a while, I succeeded. I had access to the corridors of power as well as the top brass of the religious establishment. But as I later found out, all of this was to no avail.

"As a matter of fact, what I was doing ran diametrically opposite to what I had been born to do. I fought against, persecuted, and tried to destroy the very thing I was born to uphold and defend. Isn't that interesting?

"I was far advanced in my mission when I had an encounter that would change my entire life for good. My time was up; it was time for me to make a three-hundred-and sixty-degree turn back to basics. This is the way scripture described the events leading up to my *'Damascus moment'*:

> *Meanwhile, Saul was still breathing out murderous threats against the Lord's disciples. He went to the high priest and asked him for letters to the synagogues in Damascus so that if he found any there who belonged to The Way, whether men or women, he might take them as prisoners to Jerusalem.*
>
> *As he neared Damascus on his journey, suddenly a light from heaven flashed around him. He fell to the ground and heard a voice say to him, "Saul, Saul, why do you persecute me?" "Who are you, Lord?" Saul asked. "I am Jesus, whom you are persecuting," he replied. "Now get up and go into the city and you will be told what you must do."*
>
> Acts 9:1-6 (NIV)

"This moment became the defining moment of my entire life. It was almost as if my Creator had been watching me all along waiting to see whether I would recognise my life's purpose. But when He noticed I was not going to do that anytime soon, He had to pull the brakes on me.

"Can you see what it means; the hardship you bring, the heartache you cause when you are not walking in your purpose?

"There is often heavenly frustration when a person is not walking in their purpose. But apart from the heavenly frustration, there is also the personal sense of unfulfilment, although your current circumstances might tell you otherwise. This explains the many expressions of frustrations, unhappiness, and unfulfilment even though people are successful according to society's standards.

"Can you begin to imagine the sense of frustration when you underutilise your potential? Can you imagine what must be going on in the Creator's mind about you? For He explicitly said that:

Before I formed you in the womb, I knew you. Before you were born I set you apart; I appointed you a prophet to the Nations.
Jeremiah 1:5 (NIV)

"And to add to this, many years before I came on the scene, King David once spoke about the sovereign purpose of God over our lives when he said that:

O Lord, you have searched me and you know me. You know when I sit and when I arise; you perceive my thoughts from afar.
You discern my going out and my lying down; you are familiar with all my ways ... for you created my inmost beings; you knit me together in my mother's womb. I praise you because I am fearfully and wonderfully made"
Psalm 139:1-3, 13-14 (NIV)

"When I was made to understand that my entire life course was to proclaim the gospel of God's grace to the Jews, but in particular, to the Gentiles, my entire outlook and paradigm began to change dramatically. That is what purpose can accomplish in your life."

With those words, we begin to feel we have more of the puzzle pieces for our lives to be complete. We are filled with so much confidence that we are determined to succeed in life!

Then Paul continues, "So, how can I find my life's purpose you ask? Finding your purpose has always been easy to do. Sadly though, many people have not really found the time to do so.

"To find your life's purpose, all you have to do is to ask the one who created you and thus put your purpose in you. James, one of Jesus's disciples, shows us the way to find out what our life's purpose is:

If any of you lacks wisdom, he should ask God, who gives generously to all without finding faults and it shall be given to him. But when he ask, he must believe and not doubt because he who doubts is like a wave of the sea, blown and tossed by the wind. That man should not think he will receive anything from the Lord.
James 1:5-8 (NIV)

"You don't need to be a rocket scientist to notice the opportunity you have been given to step into what God has called you to do. All you have to do is ask! Ask in prayer, and He will begin to unfold his original plan and purpose for your life. This is the key to either a life of average, mediocrity, frustration, and unfulfilment or a brand new life of purpose, energy, excitement, and a sense of fulfilment. The question now is: Which one will you choose?

"The rest of my story belongs to history, but suffice me to say at this point that this upward turnaround made a whole world of difference to my life. When I made the choice to step into all that God had for me, I found a new lease on life. It was almost as if I had entered into my mother's womb and been born again.

"Suddenly, I found incredible confidence and boldness to declare without fear or favour, the uncompromised gospel of Jesus' finished work on the cross.

"I tapped into the enormous gifts and talents God had already given me, although I hadn't noticed. I was prepared to lay my life on the line to defend the gospel. I became the incredible public face of the Christian faith better than all the public relations men and women the world could muster.

"Authority and an incredible gift of communication were made available to me. Nothing else mattered to me except preaching and teaching about Christ being crucified and the enormous freedom it presented those who would believe."

We feel an incredible sense of power and satisfaction on Paul's face as he shares what is to be the last word on what has been an incredible journey.

But before he releases us into our race, he shares these wisdom keys on how one's life purpose can make all the difference between life and death situations:

Purpose brings you in sync with your gifts and talents.

"Prior to this period, I had been well-educated in Judaism, but that was no match for the gifts and talents about to be released into my life. When I had my Damascus moment, God opened my eyes to the incredible gifts and talents he had deposited in me before the Earth's foundations.

"You mentioned communication and great oratory skills, but I did not know I had these gifts even after all the years of education.

"Similarly, when you find your purpose and what you have been born to do, there will be a release of heavenly resources in the form of natural abilities and talents that will be used to accomplish the assignment you have been given. Always remember this!"

Purpose realigns your perceptions, outlooks, and paradigms.

"Prior to my Damascus moment, I had a different outlook and paradigm about life and in particular towards Christians. Being a direct descendant of the Jews who are the remnants from whom Jesus Christ was born, my fellow country folks and I had this superior attitude about people or those we would call outsiders—the Gentiles.

"This was reflected in our opinions to the theology and doctrines of the Christian faith. In fact, I was totally convinced that Christians were heretics and that the honour of the Lord demanded their extermination, hence my zeal in bringing them to justice.

"But when I realised that all I had believed in was a lie and that my life's purpose had been to live out and defend this 'heretic' theology which is the true gospel of Jesus Christ to the Gentiles, my paradigm as well as my entire outlook on life shifted. I had to undergo a period of de-programming and re-programming in order to catch on to the heavenly vision.

"I had also realised among other things, that these people whom I had considered to be inferior were no different from me. We were all the work of a loving father who, out of his unconditional love, gave us another chance so that we can spend the rest of our lives in peace. Catching on to this revelation fired me up to want to do more. The gospel took on a whole new meaning for me.

"I was prepared to be martyred for the sake of the gospel. Today, you are enjoying the fruit of this new life because I found purpose which brought a shift in the way I looked at things."

Purpose gives you the stamina for what lies ahead.

"Your generation is filled with people who often lack stamina. This is because a lot of people have no sense of purpose or vision. People in such situations live life by default. They go anywhere the wind blows them.

"And the result? They often live lives unfulfilled, blaming society for their predicament. This is not what happened to me. Contrary to people in your generation, finding my life's calling gave me the staying power for the many uncertainties I rode on. And there were so many of them, time will not permit me to enumerate them."

"The prison cell has been my home on several occasions. Interestingly, from the prison cell, I was affecting and influencing lives with the truth of the gospel on the outside world. Can you believe this?

"The letters of encouragement I often wrote like the one to the church in Philippi, I wrote it entirely from the prison cell. Even while I was in prison, my testimony and life story influenced the wardens and some of my cell mates in such a way that they gave their lives to the God I served for whom I was in prison. There were even those who sought to prolong my stay in jail by spreading rumours and lies about me.

"But rather than cause trouble for me, the work of the gospel was further advanced as a result of it."

Philippians 1:12

Living a life of purpose attracts enemies who do not understand what you are about.

"You see, I went through a lot of hardships, pain, and warfare. These came mainly from those who did not understand what I was about. They included my fellow Jews who sought to discredit everything God was about. They often thought that opposing me was all that was needed to kill the vision God had given me. What they did not realise was that I was a pawn in the hands of God for the accomplishment of his overall plan and purpose for mankind.

"This is why they tried as hard as they could, but could not succeed. Unlike them, I had divine backing from above. I was typically fried in a boiling oil, beaten several times, shipwrecked, physically heckled, and abused by members of my heritage just to mention a few.

"Similarly, you must also take note that when you step into your purpose, there will be those who will oppose you, heckle and abuse you with every fibre of their being. Take heart because it is often a sign to show that you are walking on the right path."

Purpose finds a way of harnessing all that you have.

"When I stepped into my purpose, I thought it signalled the end of all the knowledge, education, and privileges I had. I was about to start all over again. Little did I know that I was going to use all that I had learnt in the past for the assignment ahead.

"In fact, looking back on it, it was clear that God was right there with me as I learnt and acquired knowledge. He also knew my unique heritage and upbringing was going to help with the assignment he had in mind for me.

"My unique insight and knowledge into the Greek culture, coupled with my Roman citizenship and the Jewish religion, served the overall purpose of exposing my target audience (the Gentiles) to the gospel.

"In addition to this, my training and expertise in tent-making came in handy during my missionary journeys. It enabled me the opportunity to be self-sufficient while at the same time focusing on the primary responsibility of sharing the gospel to the Gentiles.

"You are going to need every experience, talent, and expertise in order to successfully carry out your divine assignment. Even if the experiences have been bitter, they are there to serve as a morale booster so that you can change the lives of people and destinies of communities and nations."

Purpose is for the common good.

"It was God's overall agenda to bring to humanity the mystery of His work represented in Jesus Christ's sacrificial death on the cross. It was his intention that we be reconciled to Him and to the way things were at creation. This is why He chose me.

"And because I heeded to the heavenly vision, today millions of people are being brought into the family of God's children. As a result of what I was able to do, we are still claiming what is rightfully ours; what was stolen from us at creation when our ancestors, Adam and Eve, surrendered our authority to the enemy, Satan.

"And the interesting thing right now is that the reconciliatory work is still in progress. As a matter of fact, it will not stop until everyone receives this incredible gift of reconciliation. And this is all possible because I obeyed and put my hands to the plough. I say all of these things with great gratitude that God could use me to further His kingdom.

"When you step into your purpose, your obedience automatically frees others to also step into the immeasurable love and wealth God has laid out for them. Don't forget this!"

At this point, we are speechless; such a powerful testimony of a life with purpose. This is what we all yearn for. This is what Tim and many more in the world are seeking. In fact, humanity is yearning for a life of significance, a life such as the one we have just heard described to us.

How privileged and blessed we are to have received these parting words of wisdom from such a giant of the faith. This is it! Time to run onto the tracks and begin the journey.

Before Paul leaves us, he touches our shoulders and releases us into our purposes by praying for us:

Thank you, Jesus, for these precious young men and women. Remind them always of your love for them. Remind them of your purpose for their lives and help them to shake off the negative stereotypes they have often been noted for. Give them courage to run with perseverance the race you have set before them.

I have no doubt they are destined to succeed. Thank you in your precious name, AMEN!

And with this prayer, he releases us into our purpose and makes his way out. Just as it was in the beginning when we first started on this journey of encouragement, there's a standing ovation for the Apostle of the faith. But this time, he also offers applause to all the masters who have come in and spoken into our lives.

In Summary

This is what Paul the Apostle wants you to know about living today from his life experience:
- We all have our *Damascus moments*. This is when we refocus our attention to what really

matters. Don't fret when you go through it. It is only going to make you a better, fulfilled person.
- Sometimes, because of lack of purpose, we end up fighting the very thing we were created to do.
- Purpose brings you in sync with your gifts and talents.
- Purpose realigns your perceptions, outlooks, and paradigms.
- Purpose gives you the stamina for what lies ahead.
- Living a life of purpose attracts enemies who do not understand what you are about.
- Purpose finds a way of harnessing all that you have.
- Purpose is for the common good

Chapter Fifteen: Equipped for Life

It has been an incredible journey over the last twelve chapters—a journey in which so much has been said and so much has been given. This is what we need to live purposeful lives today.

For the Tim of the world, Paul assures us there's a divine assignment to fulfil where we will not succumb to the world's agenda placed upon us. Paul assures us that when we ask the Creator of our lives about our purpose, He will show us and even takes our hands as we gather the courage to step into our divine purpose. For the "Tim" of this world, there is still hope in finding your true life's calling.

Jabez also reaffirms our convictions that we can rewrite the scripts of our lives. To Sarah, he says she can turn her life around despite the odds stacked firmly against her. The secret, he says, is in discovering the power and efficacy of prayer and the confession of our faith. There is still hope out there.

These in the cloud of witnesses have taught us through their life stories, pain, and heartbreaks that in a world often plagued with frustrations and disillusionment, it is possible for one to find joy unspeakable; meaning, and purpose in life.

In the twenty-first century, post-modern, post-Christian world, there is still a lot we can learn from people who lived many centuries before us, but whose life stories provide us with incredible wisdom and courage for our time. We should not take them for granted.

They've also taught us there is still a lot we can do about living in our modern day; to change our generation armed with these powerful revelations and insights we have received from these heroes of the faith.

It is all there for us to exercise dominion and control. The question now is: What are we going to do?

Are we going to allow the same old lack of fulfilment to invade our lives? Are we going to constantly remind ourselves of all the reasons why we think we've not got what it takes to run with perseverance the race set before us?

With such a great cloud of witnesses, we have every opportunity to rise above our present circumstances so we can live fruitful and victorious lives.

After these encounters, we're confident our lives will be changed forever. We are no longer who we thought we were prior to our encounters with these great men and women of the faith.

Through them, important lessons have been passed on to us which makes it easier to navigate through life.

It is now our responsibility to set out for battle—the battle of running with perseverance the race of life. And not just to run the race, but also to make sure we run and finish it successfully.

We can certainly win the race because we are in the position to do so, having been greatly encouraged. And remember that when you lose your momentum, that is when you need to recharge your batteries and move on, not the time to throw in the towel.

This, in a nutshell, is what the ancient men and women want you to know about living today. This, without a doubt, far outweighs what the world has for so long dished out to many of us, especially to the younger generations.

And judging from the reactions as well as what we have heard, they have delivered when it matters and we have been inspired to run our race of life.

Remember, as you do life and navigate your way through this maze, you are never alone. There are many men and women cheering you on, and in many cases, are on hand to offer advice, inspiration, and the needed pep-talk to help you run with perseverance the race set before you.

You are never alone!

ABOUT THE AUTHOR

Emmanuel Donkor is an Author, Speaker, Trainer and Youth Leader who is passionate about calling out the emerging generation to deploy their potential for a more fulfilling life. He believes that a life lived with purpose is usually one that is lived when we add value to others by serving them.

He believes that a life that is well lived is when one devotes themselves to adding value to other people and this is done by serving. Thus, a life of purpose is one lived when we are of service to others. When we start to serve one another that is when a higher call to purpose is placed on us. This is why he has devoted his life to serving his generation and the next one by adding value to them through offering his expertise, experiences as well as mentoring.

Also known as 'Manny', Emmanuel has a bachelor's degree in English and Theatre Arts from the University of Ghana and a Master's degree in Communications from Westminster University in London. In addition to these, he also has a certificate in Christian Entrepreneurship from the Joseph Business School, London at the Dominion Centre in Wood Green, North London where he was adjudged the best student at the class of 2014.

Manny also has a certificate of English Language Teaching to Adults (CELTA) awarded by Cambridge University where he currently lives. This has enabled him to teach English as a foreign language (EFL) to many learners from all over the world for over 7 years mainly in London and Cambridge as his passion is teaching, training and learning and development. He is currently a student member of the Chartered Institute of Personnel and Development (CIPD) UK with a special interest in Learning and Development (L&D). He hopes to use the skills and training from CIPD to help equip businesses and organizations skill up their workforce in the Knowledge Economy.

As a day job, he is a corporate trainer and facilitator at Cambridge University Hospital Hospitals NHS Foundation Trust where he is part of a team that is responsible for the career and professional development of the thirteen thousand strong workforce.

www.ingramcontent.com/pod-product-compliance
Lightning Source LLC
Chambersburg PA
CBHW062057290426
44110CB00022B/2623